Treasures of
ANCIENT ROME

Treasures of
ANCIENT ROME

Peter Clayton

Crescent Books
New York/Avenel, New Jersey

This 1995 edition published by Crescent Books, distributed by Random House Value Publishing, Inc., 40 Engelhard Avenue, Avenel, New Jersey 07001

Random House
New York · Toronto · London · Sydney · Auckland

Produced by Brompton Books Corporation, 15 Sherwood Place, Greenwich, Connecticut 06830

ISBN 0-517-10296-X

8 7 6 5 4 3 2 1

Printed and bound in China

Page 1 : A compassionate study in bronze of a young boy dealing with the problem of a thorn in his foot – The 'Spinario.' Capitoline Museum, Rome.

Page 2–3 : Children in a Roman religious procession, a wall-painting from Ostia. Vatican Museum.

Below : A light-hearted view of the spills and thrills of the chariot race in the circus is taken on this sarcophagus relief where cupids are the contestants, chariots break down and crash and one cupid has his hand to his head in dismay at the destruction. Museo Nazionale, Naples.

Contents

Outline Chronology of Rome & Her Emperors

THE REPUBLIC

BC

753 Traditional date for the founding of Rome

625-600 Etruscan takeover of Rome

c. **534** Tarquinius Superbus becomes King of Rome

c. **509** Last Etruscan king expelled. Establishment of the Republic. Temple of Jupiter dedicated on Capitoline

c. **496** Battle of Lake Regillus against Latin League. Legendary appearance of the Dioscuri in the Forum

c. **477** Defeat of Romans and Fabian gens at Cremona

451-50 Codification of the law (The Twelve Tables)

445 Lex Canuleia

396 Fall of Veii

387 Gauls sack Rome

378 Defensive wall of Rome built

343-290 Samnite and Latin wars

280-75 War against Pyrrhus and the Greek cities of South Italy

c. **269** Beginning of Roman silver coinage

264-41 First Punic war

241 First overseas province set up in Sicily

235 Temple of Janus closed

225 Gauls defeated at Telamon

218-201 Second Punic war

217 Carthaginians win battle of Lake Trasimene

200-168 Macedonian wars

196 'Freedom' of Greece by Flamininus

168 Aemillius Paulus defeats Perseus at battle of Pydna

149-46 Third Punic war

146 Carthage and Corinth razed to the ground

142 First bridge over Tiber built

133, 123-2 Tribunates of Tiberius and Gaius Gracchus

96 Ptolemy wills Cyrene to Rome

91-87 Social war

81 Dictatorship of Sulla at Rome

74 Cyrene made a province

73-71 Slave revolt of Spartacus

66-63 Pompey's campaigns in the East

60 First Triumvirate of Pompey, Crassus and Caesar

58-51 Caesar's Gallic war

55 & 54 Caesar's expedition to Britain

49-45 Civil war

44 Dictatorship of Caesar, and his assassination on Ides of March

43 Second Triumvirate of Antony, Octavian and Lepidus

36-30 Civil war

31 Battle of Actium, 2 September, won by Octavian

30 Deaths of Antony and Cleopatra. Egypt made part of Empire but is the personal estate of the emperor

THE EMPIRE

27 Octavian hailed as Augustus, becomes first Emperor and founder of the **Julio-Claudian dynasty** (*w.* Empress Livia)

AD

9 Defeat of 3 legions in Germany under Varrus

14 Death of Augustus

14-37 Tiberius

37-41 Gaius Caligula

41-54 Claudius

41-6 Resumption of expansion with conquests of Britain, Mauretania and Thrace

43 Britain becomes part of the Empire

54-68 Nero

66-70 First Jewish revolt

68-9 Civil war. Brief reigns by Galba, Otho and Vitellius. Vespasian, first of the **Flavian dynasty**, ultimately victorious

69-79 Vespasian

79-81 Titus

79 Vesuvius erupts, destroying Pompeii and Herculaneum

80 Colosseum inaugurated

81-96 Domitian, last of the Flavians

96-8 Nerva – the **Adoptive Emperors**

98-117 Trajan

106 Dacia conquered

117 Greatest extent of Empire reached following eastern conquests

117-38 Hadrian

122 Hadrian's Wall started in Britain. Static frontiers created elsewhere

Preface

'Treasure' is probably one of the most emotive words in the English language, or in any language of the civilized world. For most people it will immediately conjure up pictures in the mind of heaps of gold and jewels and the like. Even Homer, in the *Iliad* Book IX, when he tries to give an impression of the wealth, the treasure, of the Egyptians writes, 'in Egyptian Thebes the heaps of precious ingots gleam' – yet gold in ancient Egypt was a relatively common commodity. What constitutes treasure, or a person's idea of treasure, can vary greatly. In the *Bible* (Matthew 6, 19–21), Christ says, 'Lay not up for yourselves treasures upon earth, where moth and rust doth corrupt, and where thieves break through and steal: But lay up for yourselves treasures in heaven, where neither moth nor rust doth corrupt, and where thieves do not break through and steal: For where your treasure is, there will your heart be also.' A different concept is immediately introduced and makes us realize that treasures need not necessarily all be material things.

The treasures of ancient Rome that have survived the centuries down to our own times are, similarly, not all material or solid objects. Among the nontangible 'treasures' that we have inherited from Rome, just to list a few, gives us some idea of what we 'moderns' owe to Rome: many aspects of our legal systems; literature and epic poetry; influences that permeate through the ideas of writers, artists, lawyers and so on; our style of representation of the monarch on coins; the very structure of our society and many of its moral, religious and secular tenets. In a book which is endeavoring to be objective about the treasures of ancient Rome, we can only examine those very objective and material remains that have survived. Considering the almost two thousand year gap, longer if we look back into the Roman Republic, it is quite amazing that anything at all has survived the centuries of 'moth and rust,' warfare and different political institutions and countries that have superceded the world of Rome.

How, one wonders, in the light of this have such things survived? The answer, in the main, is by chance. Many of the things that we instinctively recognize as treasure, the gold and silver plate, the jewellery and coins, fall into the category of 'buried treasure,' having been hidden away in the ground either by its rightful owner, or by a thief, and never recovered, no doubt because the person who hid it did so for a pressing reason and subsequently met an untimely end, never returning to retrieve their hoard. Invariably such hoards are found by chance, rarely by controlled excavation by archaeologists. Some of these items make their way to museums, such as the treasures from Water Newton, Kaiseraugst, Thetford and Hildesheim. Other such finds may have been overcome by disaster,

like the silver plate from the House of the Menander or Boscoreale at Pompeii. Some objects were treasured possessions that accompanied their owner to the grave and into the next world, like the silver drinking cups from graves at Welwyn and Hoby, or the Roman bronze objects and glass buried with a woman at Juellinge, Denmark, in a grave far beyond the frontiers of Imperial Rome.

In some instances superb examples of Roman craftsmanship have never been lost to view. They tend to be

the objects that have survived in the great cathedral treasuries of Europe where, by the addition of appropriate mounts, they have been translated and transformed from a pagan object into a masterpiece for Christian liturgical use. Great gemstones from the classical world were set into splendid gold chalices; in the Treasury of San Marco, Venice, for example, two marvellous chalices were made out of sardonyx cups in the tenth century under the Byzantine emperor Romanus (one dating originally from the first century BC/AD and the other from the third or fourth century AD). A glass *situla* (bucket), beautifully cut with pagan Dionysiac scenes and probably made in Rome or Alexandria in the fourth century AD had later silver

and bronze mounts added that turned it into a respectable and acceptable church vessel.

It will therefore be readily apparent that the treasures of ancient Rome, the material remains, cover very many aspects of Roman art and technology. The choice, despite the interval of some two thousand years, is still a rich one and a difficult one. Not everyone's idea of 'treasure' is the same, but an endeavor is made here to present and describe a sufficient selection of well-known and not so well-known items, buildings and places, to conjure up some idea of those treasures of ancient Rome where we now stand as their inheritors and their guardians.

P.A.C.

All pictures: In the grave of a woman in her thirties, excavated at Juellinge, Laaland, Denmark, were rich grave goods far beyond the Imperial frontiers. Round about her were her dress ornaments, long gold-headed silver hairpins, two gold beads, four silver brooches, and so on. In her right hand she holds a bronze wine-strainer and elsewhere in the grave were a pair of Roman cut-glass beakers, a bronze cauldron, ladles, bronze shears and a knife as well as other objects from the Roman world.

The Capitol at Ostia, the port of
Rome, seen from the forum.

1. The Age of Rome

'Rome,' as the old saying wisely observes, 'was not built in a day.' But then Rome lasted for many a long day, from the mid-eighth century BC (if the legends are to be believed) until almost the end of the fifth century AD when the Roman empire in the West collapsed. An even longer time span is involved if the Eastern Roman or Byzantine empire is also included because that held out until the last emperor, Constantine XI, was killed before the walls of Constantinople on 29 May 1453, defending the city against Islam and Muhammad the Conqueror. Here, however, we are only concerned with Rome until the fall of the Western Empire in AD 476.

The origins of Rome go back into the mists of legend, but archaeological excavations have now shown there to be an element of truth in those legends, or at least the dates involved. The year of the foundation of Rome is usually given as 753 BC, but of course that date is based on a later Christian event. Roman reckoning counted forward from the foundation, so their dating was *auc* (*ab urbe condita* – 'from the founding of the City'). The legend, recounted by the Roman historian Livy, tells how a Vestal Virgin gave birth to twin boys. Although she maintained that the god Mars was the father, she was imprisoned because she had broken her vows of chastity and the babies ordered to be drowned. The men supposed to carry out the deed left the twins exposed in a basket at the edge of the flooded Tiber. There, a she-wolf found them and nourished them; a shepherd named Faustulus saw her licking them and took them to his hut where he and his wife, Laurentia, raised them. The she-wolf suckling the twins, named Romulus and Remus, became a favorite motif in Roman art and a moneyer later on in the Republic, who claimed the shepherd Faustulus as an ancestor, even had the scene of their being found represented on the silver coins (denarii) struck under his control.

The boys, obvious leaders, grew to manhood with little to choose between them. One day, however, Remus mocked his brother Romulus, who was busy building walls for a new settlement. He jumped, jeering, over the half-built walls and Romulus killed him in a fit of rage. Romulus became sole king, the settlement took his name and Rome began its long climb to world mastery.

The other legend of the founding of Rome, recounted by the poet Virgil in the *Aeneid*, tells how Aeneas, a Trojan hero, fled from the sack of Troy carrying his old father Anchises on his shoulders, leading his small son Ascanius by one hand and carrying the *palladium* (the sacred images) in his other. After various adventures, including going to North Africa where Dido the queen of Carthage fell in love with him, he arrived in Latium and, having been told by his father of Rome's future great destiny, founded the city. Once again, elements of the story were often reproduced in Roman art. Several episodes make up the pattern of scenes in a great

Below: Miniature showing Aeneas received by King Latinus. Codex Vaticanus Latinus 3225. Bibl. Apostolica Vaticano.

Right: Reverse of a silver denarius of Julius Caesar showing Aeneas carrying his aged father Anchises to safety from the sack of Troy – an allusion to the foundation and ancestors of the Julian gens. British Museum, London.

Right: On one face of an altar from Ostia appear all the major elements of Roman legendary symbolism: the Dioscuri (Castor and Pollux); the imperial eagle; the Wolf and Twins, and the Tiber. Museo delle Terme, Rome.

mosaic found in a Roman bath suite at Low Ham, Somerset; Julius Caesar showed Aeneas escaping from Troy on the reverse of one of his silver denarius coins because his family, the Julii, claimed descent from Aeneas. One of the earliest literary treasures that survives from the Roman empire is an illustrated manuscript of Virgil's great poem, written about AD 400.

The legends obviously glorified the origins of Rome but at least the eighth-century BC date for the beginnings of settlement in the area that we now know as Rome seems to be quite accurate. The first settlement was a primitive affair, small groups of farmers building their huts on the higher ground. A group of such huts has been excavated on the Palatine Hill, close to the spot where Romulus was supposed to have built and

where later, under Imperial Rome, the great palaces of the emperors were to be built. The shape of these early huts can be reconstructed from the post holes left by their timbers, and we know what they looked like from the very distinctive pottery hut urns that have been excavated from the cemeteries. These small urns housed the last remains of the dead as their larger counterparts had housed the living.

Excavations deep below the later levels in the Roman Forum close to the Curia (Senate House) in 1899 revealed a black marble pavement, the Lapis Niger, which tradition said marked the site of Romulus' tomb or that of his foster father, the shepherd Faustulus. No tomb was found but of great importance, and perhaps one of the greatest and yet possibly most insignificant-looking treasures of Rome, was a square block or stele inscribed on all four sides. It dates from the sixth or early fifth centuries BC and represents the earliest example extant of the Latin language. Still not fully understood, the inscription apparently is a warning that the area is a sacred place; certainly the numerous remains of sacrifices and bronze and terracotta offerings found close by it would indicate this.

From Romulus (who died in 717/716 BC according to legend) descended a long line of kings. The little settlement on the hill expanded to take in others of the famous Seven Hills, nearby settlements and cities were conquered and brought under the sway of Rome. The last of the kings was Tarquinius Superbus (*circa* 534–509 BC) who traditionally was driven out by Lucius Junius Brutus and the Republic founded. Many years later another Brutus, claiming descent, is more famous as the assassin of Julius Caesar in 44 BC. He commemorated both events in the family history with the issue of silver coins.

The early years of the young Republic are a long tale of cities attacked and made subservient to Rome and battles against the other tribes of Italy. Some stand out, such as the battle of Lake Regillus in 496 against the Tarquins and the Latium league when the heavenly twins, Castor and Pollux, the Dioscuri, were said to have appeared on the Roman side, which was naturally victorious. Immediately after the victory they were supposedly seen watering their horses in the *Lacus Juturnae* (Basin of Juturna) in the Roman Forum where, 12 years later, a temple was raised on its east side in their honor by Aulus Postumius. In 396 Rome plucked a persistent thorn from her side when she overcame and captured the nearby Etruscan city of Veii, removing an ever-present threat. Six years later the tables were turned when the Gauls swept down Italy and attacked Rome. The Capitol, seat of the city's tutelary gods, was fortified for a last stand; all able-bodied men were to form its garrison and take in the women and children. It was agreed that those too infirm or elderly to be of use would remain outside. The story goes that the older senators and men of distinction decided to meet their end with dignity, dressed in

their finest official robes. This they did and stood in silent ranks to meet the rampaging Gauls who, in their turn, stopped in amazement, gazing at these resplendently dressed, still and aloof old men arrayed before them. They thought that they were in some holy place but the spell was broken when one Gaul, a little braver or less in awe than the rest, reached out and touched the long beard of a certain Marcus Papirius, who promptly hit him on the head with his ivory staff of office. They were slain where they stood, houses were sacked and the city set on fire. The Capitol garrison still held out and was only saved from a surprise night attack of the Gauls, silently climbing the steep rocks of the fortress, by the cackling of the geese sacred to the goddess Juno. Their sanctity had saved them from becoming emergency rations for the defenders, and they in turn saved the beleaguered Romans. One sentry, charged with negligence on duty, was summarily sentenced and hurled to his death from the top of the rock. The garrison held out for seven months until eventually famine drove them to capitulate and ransom themselves with gold. As soon as the Gauls had the golden loot they withdrew, but they were back three years later in 387, when they captured the city.

Left: The Lapis Niger with its inscription in archaic script, now located beneath the present ground level in the Forum at Rome.

Coins, from left to right: Julius Caesar was the first living Roman to appear on the coinage of Rome; it was a short-lived issue. Silver denarius. British Museum, London.

Silver denarius of Brutus, one of Caesar's assassins. It shows a portrait of Brutus and the reverse has two daggers and a priestly cap (symbol of Caesar's office of High Priest (Pontifex Maximus)) with the date of the Ides of March. British Museum, London.

Cleopatra VII. the last queen and reigning Ptolemy of Egypt, on a silver tetradrachm struck at Ascalon. Considered to be the finest known specimen of this coin. Private collection.

In the fourth and third centuries BC, Rome was busy fighting against neighboring tribes (there were three Samnite wars), the Etruscans and also further afield with her former ally Carthage in North Africa (there were three Punic wars). The conflicts swayed backward and forward with Rome occasionally being beaten; for example by the Samnites in 315 at Lautulae; by Pyrrhus of Epirus with his elephants at Heraclea in 280; by the Carthaginians at Lake Trasimene in 217 and again in 216 at Cannae. However, Roman defeats were few compared to Roman victories. Polybius (*circa* 200–118 BC), the Greek statesman and historian, wrote about the early history of Rome and noted that Rome achieved its supremacy in just 53 years (from the start of the Second Punic War in 220 down to 167 BC, after the battle of Pydna). 'The supremacy,' he wrote, 'of the Romans did not come about, as certain Greek writers have supposed, either by chance or without the victors knowing what they were doing. On the contrary, since the Romans deliberately chose to school themselves in such great enterprises, it is quite natural that they should not only have boldly embarked upon their pursuit of universal dominion, but that they should actually have achieved their purpose.' Polybius certainly knew from first-hand experience what he was writing about, for 16 years after the defeat of Macedon at Pydna he was kept a virtual but honored prisoner in Rome without any accusations being brought against him or trial. Fortunately he befriended the son of the victor of the battle of Pydna and his sojourn in Rome is best described as a loose 'house arrest.' He met and mixed with the aristocracy and was accepted because of his similar military and statesmanlike background. His *Histories* is one of the most valuable and accurate sources for Roman history from 220–145 BC. All the while Rome was extending its rule outward from beside the Tiber and was much concerned with lawmaking rather than building. The first stone bridge over the Tiber was only built in 142 BC. Perhaps one of Rome's greatest conquests in the Republican period was that of Greece in 196 – 'the Freedom of Greece' the Romans

preferred to call it. It was commemorated on an extremely rare gold coin, a stater, carrying the portrait of the victorious general Flamininus. He was the first living Roman to appear on a coin, a Greek coin, while Julius Caesar, 152 years later, was the first living Roman to appear on a Roman coin.

Such was the power now of Rome that several Hellenistic monarchs, in an endeavor to save their people hardship as a conquered nation, willed their country to Rome, for example Nicomedes IV bequeathed Bithynia to Rome in 74 BC. This ruse did not always work, as Boudica of the Iceni in Britain found out when her husband Prasutagus died, leaving half his estate to Rome. Rome wanted it all, no half measures. Caesar came to land on British shores twice, in 55 and 54 BC but it was a hundred years later that the legions landed in force and made Britain part of the empire in AD 43. Before that the late Republic went through a series of shocks. One of the greatest defeats it suffered up to that point in its history, more to morale really than anything else, was when the general Crassus was defeated at Carrhae in Mesopotamia; of his 35,000 men a mere 10,000 survived and he lost his own life and the legionary standards to the Parthian army of about 10,000 mounted archers. It was to be many years before those standards were to be regained.

Despite all these events, covering some 700 years, Rome had little to show for it in terms of material treasures, buildings and objects, that can be securely dated to the period. Perhaps her greatest 'treasure' was the legal system and the many laws that were formulated and laid down. In the later years of the first century BC there is a change from the Republic to what is called the Imperatorial period, beginning really when Caesar made his famous crossing of the river Rubicon at the head of an army into Italian territory in 50 BC. It is these years, in the third quarter of the last century BC, that are perhaps best known generally, notably for the murder of Caesar on the Ides of March (15th) in 44 BC. Caesar had only recently been voted Dictator for life when he fell to the assassins' daggers. His principal murderer, Brutus, was killed at the battle of Philippi in 42 BC by troops led by Octavian, Caesar's avenging nephew and adopted son. The power struggle continued and culminated with the sea battle at Actium in Greek waters on 2 September 31 BC. Here a fleet led by Antony and Cleopatra met a smaller fleet led by Octavian. Accounts vary as to exactly what happened, suffice it that Cleopatra, followed by Antony, put out to sea and made for Egypt where first she and then Antony committed suicide. Octavian was master of the Roman world and marched into Egyptian Alexandria on 1 August 30 BC. Three years later, in 27 BC, he changed his name to Augustus and founded the Roman Empire or Imperial period. Had he not been so fortunate at Actium, if the battle had swung the other way, there would have been no Roman empire to act as a foundation for so many present-day European institutions; the emphasis then and in our later culture would have been more eastern Mediterranean – 'oriental' – in character. Augustus (Octavian), by becoming the first Roman emperor, brought a stability to the Empire while still maintaining the fiction that it was still a Republic but, much as many might hark back to it, it was dead. At least Rome's first emperor laid a good foundation in his long reign (27 BC–AD 14) and died in his bed, both things that many of his successors would have envied him.

The history of Rome after Augustus falls into fairly specific groupings of emperors – dynasties is not quite the correct description of Rome in every instance, but it is a convenient one. It is within these divisions that it is possible, in many instances, to be far more specific in assigning certain features, buildings, artefacts and so on because they are themselves a reflection of the period and its events. Augustus' successors, the Julio-Claudian dynasty, reigned until the suicide of Nero on 9 June AD 68. The period was one of fine buildings, beautifully designed and made objects from the most precious materials to the most mundane, as will be seen later. With Nero's death, there began a struggle for supremacy, for 'the purple,' and AD 68 has become known as 'the year of the four emperors' – Nero, Galba, Otho and Vitellius. They died, alternately, by suicide and murder. In AD 69, Vespasian, an army general, inaugurated the Flavian dynasty (Flavius was the family name), and was followed by his two sons, Titus and Domitian. In this short period of 17 years occurred the First Jewish Revolt, the destruction of Pompeii and Herculaneum by Vesuvius in AD 79 and the inauguration of the Flavian amphitheater (more popularly known as the Colosseum) in AD 80.

The following groups of emperors are known collectively as the Adoptive Emperors, AD 96–197, although not all were actually adopted by their predecessors. During this period, in the reign of Trajan (98–117), the Roman Empire reached its greatest extent, encompassing many different countries and people, with different backgrounds and histories. It is small wonder

Above: The great gold medallion found at Arras, Pas de Calais, in 1922. It refers to the reconquest of Britain by Constantius Chlorus in AD 296 and is one of the most important historical Roman coins that has survived. Arras Museum, France.

that many of the surviving buildings and artefacts show many influences. After the death of Didius Julianus (who had 'purchased' the empire by offering to pay 25,000 sestertii to each soldier), Septimius Severus, governor of Syria, was proclaimed emperor and inaugurated the Severan dynasty. As Severus was a native of North Africa (he was born in Leptis Magna, in AD 146) there is an understandable emphasis on building in the great towns of the province, many still extant today as magnificent ruins. The Severan dynasty was followed by the Age of Military Anarchy, AD 235–285, when in the short space of 50 years no less than 34 emperors ruled. The reigns of many were very short, a few months or, in some instances, a matter of only three weeks. Despite the rapidity of their removal

from their high office they all managed to strike coins bearing their portraits. Obviously many of them today are extremely rare pieces, but they do at least show the emperor when often little else is known about him.

In the late third century there were troubles in many parts of the empire, individuals breaking away from the City (better known nowadays as UDI!). Referred to as the Secessionist Empires there were three distinct areas: the Gallic Empire in Gaul and Lower Germany; the Palmyrene Empire in Syria; and the British Empire. These were all brought under control by the Jovian and Herculian Dynasties (named from the two patron gods, Jupiter and Hercules, of the joint emperors Diocletian and Maximian), and the House of Constantine. It was Constantine's father, Constantius Chlorus, who brought the secessionist British Empire back into the Roman fold in AD 296, an event commemorated on the great gold Arras medallion. Constantine I, the Great (AD 307–337), is noted for two major innovations, he made Christianity the official religion and he moved the capital in AD 330 from Rome to a new city on an old site (Byzantion) which he renamed to his own glory Constantinople. Political expediency and strategy demanded that he had a capital closer to the threatened frontiers of the empire. It was political expediency rather than any deep religious conviction that led him to proclaim Christianity the official religion of the empire. He had been converted in AD 312 after his vision prior to the battle of the Milvian Bridge when he was shown a sign (the chi-rho monogram, symbol of Christ) and told 'Hoc signo victor eris!' ('By this sign shall you conquer!'). It was duly carried into battle the next day, 28 October, on the shields of his soldiers and his adversary Maxentius perished. Although nominally a Christian, and

A sacrificial bull is led forward to the decorated stone *omphalos* (the navel of the world, sacred to Apollo at Delphi) as Apollo plays his lyre. Pompeii, House of the Vettii.

having summoned the first great church council at Nicaea (modern Iznik in Turkey) in AD 325, he was only baptized, as was the custom, on his deathbed on 22 May 337 at Ancyrona near Nicomedia.

The years that followed were troubled times, the last of the line of Constantine, his nephew a grandson of Constantius Chlorus, was Julian II, often called the Apostate since he endeavored to turn back to the old pagan gods. The year AD 364 saw what was really the beginning of the end, the last few years, of the Roman Empire in the West. Valentinian I inaugurated the House of Valentinian and the Theodosian Dynasty. It was a period that saw several usurper emperors arise again in Britain. Magnus Maximus was proclaimed emperor by his troops and reigned for almost five years. His name and legend lived on in Welsh Celtic legend as Maxen Wledig and in Rudyard Kipling's *Puck of Pook's Hill*. His son, Flavius Victor, was co-emperor with him for about a year. Honorius, one of the rightful emperors, was the one who recalled the Roman troops from Britain in AD 410, leaving the Britons to fend for themselves and the next year another usurper proclaimed himself Constantine III, associating his son Constans with him. The last emperors of the Western Empire who saw the final collapse reigned at most five years (Anthemius) but many only for a year or less. By a strange quirk of fate (Fortune or Tyche as the historian Polybius would have immediately noticed), the last emperor of the Roman West was called Romulus Augustulus – the little Augustus. He reigned a bare 10 months and the wheel of history had come full circle from Romulus to Romulus in just over 1200 years.

2. The Architectural Grandeur

The magnificently restored
three-storey stage building of the
theater at Sabratha gives an
excellent idea of how the players
must have been vastly overshadowed by its grandeur.

Perhaps one of the easiest yardsticks by which it is possible to measure the greatness of any civilization is its architecture: the basic concepts that motivated it and what remains today. Everything must start from small beginnings and Roman architecture is no exception to the rule. The first settlement on the banks of the Tiber had no architecture as such, no grand concepts, only a basic provision for the protection of its folk in small huts, the evidence for which today is largely archaeological from the pattern left by excavated post holes. Some idea of what these structures looked like can be gained from the pottery urns in which the ashes of those cremated were placed. Many of these urns took the form of the houses of the living, now converted appropriately to be the house for the dead. A development may be seen in these hut urns, leading on to finer examples with gabled roofs and other refinements. As in most civilized communities a place would have been set aside for a temple to the deity that protected the people, and where the inhabitants could make the appropriate offerings to the god or goddess in supplication for favors sought, or to placate a deity that might perhaps have shown its anger, so they thought, by natural disasters such as flood.

The Romans took over a lot from their predecessors, the Etruscans. Exactly how much of Roman civilization has an underlying base in the Etruscan will probably never be fully established because Rome made a very thorough job of eradicating as much of Etruria as possible. The Etruscans had been fine builders and engineers, erecting vast stone walls to guard their cities, excavating huge channels through solid rock to convey water and building well-proportioned temples to their gods and finely cut, carved and decorated tombs for their dead. Terracotta models reveal what the temples were like; they had heavily tiled roofs and decorated antefixes, often a Gorgon's head or grinning face, around the edge of the roof. Their fluted columns were engaged in the walls of the *cella* (shrine) and they had a decorated pediment above the entrance. This in itself was not new and owed much in the design to its predecessors, the temples of Greece. Excellent examples were, of course, still standing and in daily use in southern Italy (called Magna Graecia, Greater Greece) where Greek colonists had settled in earlier centuries and built what are some of the finest surviving examples today of Greek temples.

The architectural heritage of Republican Rome is tiny by comparison with that of Imperial Rome. It might be expected that fine buildings of this early period in Rome's expansion would be found in Rome itself but as with any great and expanding city later more grandiose buildings tend to sweep away the smaller, earlier ones. Many of the great temples of later Rome obviously stand, rebuilt, on earlier sites. The Forum itself is evidence of this, where the sacred

Above: Models in terracotta of houses and temples, the former normally used as cinerary urns, give a good idea of what the buildings of early Rome, now often only known from foundations, looked like.

Below: Group of four temples of the Republican period in the Largo Argentina, Rome. Three are rectangular and one circular.

Left : The circular temple of Vesta, close by the temple of Fortuna Virilis, dates from the first century AD and was probably dedicated to Portunus, the harbor god.

Above : The so-called temple of Fortuna Virilis, Rome, was more probably dedicated to the Mater Matuta and dates from the end of the third century BC. One of the few surviving examples of a Greco-Italian temple of the Republican period. It is a pseudo-peripteral temple with four fluted Ionic columns before the portico.

enclosure in which the Lapis Niger stood is now several feet below the Imperial Rome levels. There is a series of four temples of Republican date called the Sacra del Largo Argentina near the Corso Vittoria Emanuele. They only exist now as podiums, each with a few restored columns, in a row – the second temple is circular, the others rectangular. To which deities they were dedicated is not now known but it was behind the circular temple, in the portico of the Curia Pompei, that Caesar was murdered in 44 BC on the Ides of March.

Down by the Tiber, in the Forum Boarium, stand the two best remaining Republican temples in Rome, the delightful little round temple commonly called the temple of Vesta and the small Ionic-style temple known as Fortuna Virilis. This is the older of the two temples and dates from the late third century BC. Its dedication is more probably to the Mater Matuta than to Fortuna. The circular temple almost certainly dates from the early years of the first century AD and, like its nearby companion, has a wrong name since it was very likely dedicated to the god of harbors, Portunus, rather than Vesta, goddess of the hearth and home, whose name it has borne for centuries. Both temples survived, like so many architectural treasures that have overcome the depredations of time and the hand of man, because they were converted into Christian churches; the pseudo-peripteral temple of 'Fortuna' was consecrated as Santa Maria Egiziaca in AD 872 and its circular companion in the Middle Ages was first the church of Santo Stefano delle Carrozze and subsequently Santa Maria del Sole. Had it not been for this later, changed, religious use they would not have stood until today.

Stone buildings in Republican Rome were rare and it was left to Octavian when he became the first emperor of Rome in 27 BC as Augustus to bring about the change. The final major battle of the Imperatorial period, Actium in 31 BC, had left the balance of power well and truly with Rome. It was said of Augustus that he found Rome a city built of bricks but left it a city built of marble. The finest building extant of the period is another temple, the Pantheon, but it suffered subsequent rebuilding and restoration in antiquity. It was originally built by Augustus' son-in-law, M Vipsanius Agrippa, who had been admiral of the fleet at Actium (he had married Augustus' daughter Julia and was designated his heir, but he predeceased the emperor in 12 BC). The temple was erected to commemorate the victory at Actium and built of travertine blocks. Badly damaged in a fire in AD 80, it was restored by the emperor Domitian and then rebuilt (and probably designed) by Hadrian in brick on a larger scale. At this time it was rededicated to the seven major planetary gods but it still kept its old name of the Pantheon, the 'most holy place.' Further restorations were carried out by Septimius Severus and his son Caracalla at the turn of the second century. It was closed and ignored by the early Christian emperors in the fourth century and pillaged by the Goths in their attack on Rome. Its consecration as the Christian church Santa Maria ad Martyres in AD 609 did not stop Constans II, the

Byzantine emperor, despoiling it. He visited Rome for 12 days (5–17 July) in AD 663, the first emperor to do so in almost 200 years since the fall of the Western Roman Empire. When he left he took the gilded bronze roof tiles of the Pantheon with him. Today, better known as Santa Maria Rotonda (rather than after the 28 cart-loads of martyrs' bones said to have been transferred there from the catacombs), it is among the finest preserved and most perfect buildings surviving from ancient Rome. It now also houses the bodies of Italy's kings.

In the first century AD building went on rapidly in Rome and techniques improved; of particular value here was the Roman invention of cement, that also led to concrete, which made so many more types of building possible. Technological improvements with lifting tackle meant that larger blocks could be moved with greater ease. Carved blocks from the tomb of the Haterii found on the Via Labricana, near the Porta Maggiore, give us one of the best representations of Roman technology at work. A large crane is being worked to raise heavy blocks, presumably to finish off the roof of the highly ornate and sculpted temple beside it whose style harks back to the terracotta temple models. The hoisting is effected by a group of men working inside a huge treadmill which then gears with a windlass, ropes and a pulley at the crane's head where two workmen are perched. The relief dates to the

last years of the first century or the early second century AD. Represented on other blocks in the tomb are a series of the monuments that existed along the Via Sacra, many of them often identified by name. One block has a frontal view of an arch dedicated to the Egyptian goddess Isis. This triple-arch formed the monumental entrance to the temple of Isis and her consort Serapis that stood in the Campus Martius. Vespasian spent the night in the temple of Isis when he came to Rome from Syria to become emperor in AD 69. In commemoration of the goddess' protection he had the temple represented on a large coin, a sestertius. This, and the Haterii relief, together are the only contemporary representation of the great temple to the Egyptian goddess. Nothing now remains of the original arch which was destroyed in 1585 and 1597 in two portions.

The other building represented on the block with the arch still survives, the very epitome of Roman architecture and grandeur in the eyes of many people – the Flavian Amphitheater, more popularly known as the Colosseum. The relief shows the main entrance and staircase with gladiators in the arches of the arcades of the first storey and eagles in the second storey; the entrance is adorned with a quadriga (a two-wheeled chariot drawn by four horses abreast) driven by the emperor atop an arch. An immediately noticeable discrepancy is the fact that the Colosseum has four storeys, as it is seen today. The fourth storey dates from the reign of Severus Alexander (AD 222–235) but the earlier three storeys, in order upward from ground level, were of the Doric, Ionic and Corinthian orders. The proper name of the Colosseum, the Flavian Amphitheater, comes from the family name of the emperor

Above left : The Pantheon in Rome is one of the best preserved of all Roman monuments although it was restored by several emperors after being originally built by M. Vipsanius Agrippa, Augustus' son-in-law, in 27 BC to commemorate the victory over Antony and Cleopatra at the battle of Actium in 31 BC.

Above : A relief from the monument of the Haterii family showing slaves working a treadmill. Vatican Museum.

Below : A fragment of relief from the tomb of the Haterii represents monuments along the Via Sacra that include the Colosseum and the great arch of the temple of Isis.

Vespasian who began building it in AD 72. It was finished and dedicated by his son Titus in AD 80, a year after Vespasian's death. Its popular name comes from its colossal size, rather than a colossal statue of Nero that once stood close by. The amphitheater was built on the site of a lake in the garden of Nero's Golden House (Domus Aurea). It is eliptical in shape, 205 by 170 yards, a third of a mile in circumference and 63 yards (187 feet) high. The arena is 83 by 50 yards and surrounded by tier upon tier of seats. It probably held about 50,000 spectators who were segregated with the Roman knights occupying the lower seats, wealthier citizens in the middle and the general populace in the top rows (rather like the 'gods' in a modern concert hall or opera house). The Colosseum was designed so that this huge number of spectators could easily enter and leave by a series of 160 passages and stairways. The central area was for the spectacles presented which included gladiatorial combats and fights with wild beasts, and it could even be flooded for the presentation of mock sea battles. The last are represented on silver coins of Septimius Severus and his two sons, while the first feature became a popular form of decoration on mosaic pavements laid throughout the empire, from the amusing little cupid gladiators at the Bignor Villa in Sussex to the lifelike bloody combats represented in North Africa. There is a series of underground rooms and passageways beneath, which housed the captive animals (and people, at times) so that they could be introduced directly into the arena. The essential plan of the Colosseum was widely copied over succeeding centuries in almost every corner of the empire. Some amphitheaters still stand in the center of

Above: The Colosseum, more correctly the Flavian amphitheater, probably got its popular name from a colossal statue of Nero that stood nearby. It is a masterpiece of planning with 80 entrance arches giving access to vaulted corridors that led to the staircases giving on to the spectators' seats. It could seat an audience of about 50,000 people.

towns never abandoned since Roman times and several are still the scene of performances and presentations of classical works. Others rise majestically above tiny towns, like El Djem in Tunisia, the sixth largest example; the ampitheater commands the countryside for miles around. Viewing the great mass of the Colosseum it is difficult at times to realize that only about a third of the original building remains, the rest having been removed over the years as it was used as a convenient quarry for the buildings of medieval Rome, as well as a stronghold by the Frangipani and Annibaldi families. It was only in the mid-eighteenth century, with its dedication by Pope Benedict XIV to the Passion of Jesus and sanctified by martyrs' blood, that its wholesale destruction ceased. Some of the best contemporary representations of it appear on coins of Titus and later, in the third century, on a splendid medallic piece of Gordian III that has a three-quarters bird's-eye view that shows the entertainment with animals taking place. As the Latin poet Juvenal noted: *duos tantum res axius optat, panem et circenses* (the Roman populace were concerned only with two things, bread and circuses); the Colosseum catered for the latter in the grand manner.

The Colosseum now stands at the end of the Via dei Fori Imperiali, a thoroughfare almost 1000 yards in length which is lined with the magnificent remains of the religious and formal buildings of ancient Rome. It

Above: The east face of the Arch of Titus in the Roman Forum with its dedication to the deified emperor Vespasian and his son Titus to commemorate the conquest of Judaea and the fall of Jerusalem in AD 79. It was erected in AD 81.

Below: Relief on the interior wall of the Arch of Titus showing the spoils from the capture of Jerusalem, including the altar from Solomon's Temple and the seven-branched golden candlestick, the Menorah, symbolic of the Jewish faith.

was not always like this. In medieval times most of the buildings, now exposed for the architectural treasures that they are, were hidden and incorporated in a welter of cheek by jowl houses. In this century steady programs of clearance have revealed more and more of the ancient buildings, culminating in the opening of the Via dei Fori Imperiali in October 1933. The greatest area of remains lies on its south side, the Roman Forum proper with, beyond it, the Palatine Hill with its imperial palaces. At the Colosseum end of the Forum begins the Sacred Way into the Forum with the arch of Titus standing astride. Many arches were erected in Rome (and throughout the empire) in the course of the centuries; some, like the arch of Isis, were merely entrances to sacred areas but the majority are commemorative of great occasions, voted to an emperor illustrating his conquests – like the arch of Claudius saluting his conquest of Britain in AD 43, now only to be seen represented on the coins he struck to celebrate the event and fragments of its dedication inscription preserved in the Capitoline Museum. The arch of Titus, a simple and perfectly proportioned single archway covered in Pentelic marble, was erected in AD 81 by Domitian to honor his father's (Vespasian) and brother's (Titus) victories in the Jewish War of AD 70. The culmination of the war was the sack of the city of Jerusalem and a relief on the inside of the arch is not only of the highest historical significance, it is also perhaps the most poignant contemporary illustration relating to the Jewish faith in art. Roman soldiers triumphantly carry away the spoils from Jerusalem

Left: The Roman Forum seen from the Palatine Hill with the Arch of Septimius Severus and the Curia, Senate House, in the background.

Above: Reliefs on the Arch of Septimius Severus, seen here from the Forum, represent his victorious campaigns against the Parthians and Arabs. It was erected in AD 203.

which include the treasures of the Temple, the altar decorated with trumpets and the Menorah, the seven-branched golden candlestick. It is a matter of speculation as to what subsequently became of these objects, valued for their religious significance as well as their intrinsic worth. Legends grew up, especially about the Menorah, in medieval and later times, one of which would locate the candlestick as still concealed in southern France. The relief on the facing interior wall of the arch shows the goddess Roma guiding Titus and Victory in their triumphal chariot. The reminder that all men are mortal, although emperors become gods, occurs in the relief in the ceiling vault which shows the Apotheosis of Titus, carried to the heavens on the back of an eagle, the normal symbolism for the emperor's deification that occurs in sculpture and frequently on the 'consecratio' coins issued by their immediate successors.

From the arch of Titus, standing on a slight eminence, the Roman Forum, a veritable treasure-house of buildings, stretches away to the Capitol at the far end. Looking at all this from a vantage point or wandering among the ruins, some more grandiose or better preserved than others, it is difficult to remember that what is seen now represents only the last phase of Imperial Rome, in that buildings were being added, rebuilt and restored throughout the centuries so that given any specific point in time many of those now seen would be missing since they had not then been built. The area of the Forum is low lying, it was a marsh until it was drained in the early sixth century BC and became the meeting place for the people from the settlements on the hilltops. The great drain or sewer built then, the Cloaca Maxima, continued in use throughout the history of Rome and its outlet into the Tiber can still be seen close by one of the bridges.

The western end of the Forum was in use from the earliest times and it was here, underground and just in front of the Curia – the Senate House – that a sacred enclosure was excavated and the Lapis Niger, the earliest Latin inscription, still remains. The other great structure at this end of the Forum, almost closing it and balancing the arch of Titus at the east end, is the great triumphal arch of Septimius Severus. This is bigger and heavier than the beautifully proportioned arch of Titus of 150 years earlier. Septimius' is the more usual triple gateway arch, a central one flanked by smaller openings. Like most of the buildings in the Forum it was not placed where it is by accident, it had many political and religious overtones in its siting, being on the spot where Septimius, in a dream, had seen his predecessor Pertinax slip from a white horse that then carried Septimius up on high – an obvious portent of future glory. Also, it was close by the rostra (the orator's tribune) and the Senate House, symbolic of democratic good rule. Rare coins of Septimius Severus and of his son Caracalla show us what the arch was like originally, so that we know that there was originally a bronze six-horse chariot on top of it with statues of Severus and his sons Caracalla and Geta. It is 75 feet high and 82 feet wide. The reliefs on the arch record the emperor's victorious campaigns against the Parthians and the Arabs and the inscriptions repeat this with his many honorific titles. The arch was erected in AD 203 in association with the festivities for the tenth year of the emperor's reign. After Severus' death in AD 211 his eldest son, Caracalla, had his brother Geta murdered in AD 212 and his name was removed from the inscriptions on the arch. However, the dowel holes that held the bronze letters were not obliterated at the time and the original inscription can therefore be recovered.

The other major arch in Rome is that of Constantine I, the Great. This stands beside the Colosseum at the head of the Via di San Gregoria and is a triple arch like the earlier arch of Severus. Constantine's arch was erected to commemorate his victory over Maxentius at the battle of the Milvian Bridge three years before in AD 312. Until 1804 it was largely concealed in the medieval fortifications of the Frangipani family, who had also fortified the Colosseum. It is heavily decorated with reliefs but, curiously, few of them date from the reign of Constantine. Only the friezes above the side arches and on either end of the arch, the reliefs at the bases of the columns and those tucked into the spandrels of each archway, and the two medallions at the ends are Constantinian work. All the rest, the great medallions on each face, panels at the top and inside the archway and the eight great, over-lifesize statues of Dacians atop the columns come from other earlier monuments, mainly from the reigns of Trajan, Hadrian and Marcus Aurelius. The variation in style and quality between the two groups is very obvious. The medallions show the emperor Hadrian variously hunting lions and bears and sacrificing to Hercules and Apollo.

The Trajanic reliefs are concerned with the Dacian wars and those of Marcus Aurelius show him addressing the army, his entry into Rome and allied subjects. The quality of the work is very high and presumably each of the three original monuments represented by these reliefs must have been in a bad state of repair by the early fourth century for Constantine to reuse them. Despite the hotchpotch date of its reliefs, somehow Constantine's arch achieves a homogeneity of presentation if not style. Edward Gibbon, however, in his *Decline and Fall of the Roman Empire* took a poor view of the arch and described it as 'a melancholy proof of the decline of the arts, and a singular testimony of the meanest vanity'.

Rome itself is a vast treasure house of Roman architecture, invariably of mixed dates throughout the Imperial period and in varying conditions of preservation. Architecturally Rome is like a pebble dropped into a pond from which the ripples spread wider and wider. It is to be expected that there should be fine Roman architectural remains in Italy and many closely parallel monuments in Rome, for example, the arches of Trajan at Ancona and at Benevento both look to the

arch of Titus for their inspiration and simplicity and many amphitheaters have their origin in the Colosseum.

Domestic architecture can be seen from the shops and small dwellings of Trajan's markets to the grand, largely ruined palaces on the Palatine Hill. Hadrian chose to move outside Rome for his favorite palace, and his great villa covering 12 acres is set in an imperial estate of some 180 acres 20 miles east of Rome, near Tivoli in the Alban Hills. Hadrian's villa is unique, a great treasure house not only of statues (largely dispersed in the major collections of the world since the eighteenth century) but also of architectural splendor in its ideas. It took over 10 years to build from AD 125, yet he hardly saw it or lived there owing to his incessant travelling throughout the empire and the fact that his later ill-health forced him to move south to Baiae, where he died in 138. At the villa Hadrian wanted to create those places that had most impressed him on his frequent travels. From Greece he reproduced the Academy, the Lyceum, the Prytaneum and the Stoa Poikile; from Thessaly, the Vale of Tempe; and from Egypt the Canopus mouth of the Nile. Everything was provided for the philosopher-emperor including a Latin and a Greek library, various baths, a Greek theater and a charming little retreat known as the Naval theater, a small island within a 12-foot-broad moat that could only be reached by a revolving bridge. Here probably the emperor could find peace and solitude and his two libraries were close by.

Hadrian's re-creation of the Canopus (which lay about 15 miles east of Alexandria in Egypt) consists of

Left: The fourth-century AD Arch of Constantine curiously incorporates a number of reliefs and statues from earlier, second century, monuments but nevertheless has a satisfying and balanced aspect.

Below left: Detail of the attic story of Constantine's Arch where the difference in artistic

approach in the reused second century roundels and the fourth century horizontal sculpture of the Imperial court is evident.

Below: The Canopus at Hadrian's villa, Tivoli, in the Alban foothills outside Rome. Here the emperor re-created a number of his favorite spots that he had visited in the empire.

a canal over 100 yards long with a series of rooms and a portico down one side and a heavy wall down the other against which were set entertainment booths. Under the arches stood statues of various deities and animals, even including stone crocodiles. At the apsidal end of the canal was a nymphaeum, usually referred to as the Serapeum (after the Egyptian god), and it was from this area that most of the Egyptian statues from the site now in the Vatican and Capitoline museums came. This reconstruction, of all those made at the villa, obviously had most memories for Hadrian since it was in the Nile in middle Egypt that his favorite, Antinöus, had drowned in AD 130. The grief-stricken emperor founded the city of Antinoopolis near the site of the accident in his memory, had him deified and allowed the young man's portrait to appear on coinage from many of the Greek cities in the Empire, as well as Alexandria in Egypt. The whole villa complex is a delightful area, especially with its pines, but the Canopus is even more enchanting.

Domestic architecture is best represented in Italy at three towns: Ostia the port of Rome and Pompeii and Herculaneum, both destroyed in the violent eruption of Vesuvius in August AD 79. Ostia was a bustling commercial port with a great harbor begun under Claudius and finished by Nero, who commemorated it with a delightful bird's eye view on his large orichalcum (brass) sestertii. Today it is possible to wander through the ruins of private houses, offices in the Square of Corporations with their sign-board mosaics, the great baths, the several theaters and the communal public lavatories. Invariably quiet and peaceful, it gives a much better impression of a Roman town than its more famous and tourist-ridden sisters Pompeii and Herculaneum. It is from these two towns (not the only ones destroyed in the eruption on the bay of Naples) that most of our evidence comes for the Roman way of life, town architecture (religious, public and domestic), wall paintings, mosaics and the peoples' possessions. Pompeii was destroyed by the falling lava and choking dust while Herculaneum disappeared under the thick mud that flowed down the mountainside. In a letter to the historian Tacitus the younger Pliny, who was 17 at the time and at nearby Misenum, gives a graphic eyewitness account of how for several days there had been minor earth tremors and then on 24 August a huge cloud appeared, 'like an umbrella pine,' ashes fell in heavy showers, the ground rocked and the sea was 'sucked away and apparently forced back by the earthquake: at any rate it receded from the shore so that quantities of sea creatures were left stranded on dry sand'. Great flames shot skyward and day was turned into night. Among those who died in the cataclysm was Pliny the Elder, the historian who was admiral of the fleet at the time, who went to investigate. He was obviously asphyxiated as 'his body was found intact and uninjured, still fully clothed and looking more like sleep than death.

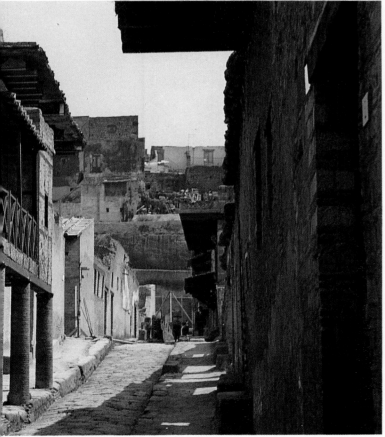

Above left: The garden of the House of the Vettii at Pompeii has been restocked with plants and shrubs to give an excellent idea of the pleasant aspect of this house of two wealthy merchant brothers.

Above: The atrium of the House of the Faun at Pompeii with a replica of the dancing faun from which it receives its name.

Left: Herculaneum, being overwhelmed by liquid mud in the eruption of AD 79, has a more natural aspect and 'lived in' atmosphere than its neighbor Pompeii, buried in ash.

The eruption sealed the towns in a time capsule and also those who did not escape. Some of the finest Roman silver plate surviving comes from this area. Architecturally there are the actual house structures as well as the mosaics and wall paintings described below. The buildings range from the great forum, official temples and upper class houses to warehouses and the smallest hovels. The houses of the wealthy inhabitants of Pompeii were tastefully laid out with atriums, shallow pools in courtyards and cool gardens. Statuary was carefully placed at vantage points and bronze statues adorned the central podium of many of the pools. The extant wall paintings often include views of houses or seaside villas and their architectural details add supplementary details to those already known from the actual buildings.

Away from Rome itself, the buried cities of the Campagna and Ostia, there are no huge complete architectural complexes and generally it is the surviv-

Right : The amphitheater at Verona is the third largest in the Roman world ; it ranks after the Colosseum and the amphitheater at Capua and could seat 22,000 spectators.

Left : Theaters from the east to the west in the Roman empire showed little difference except in size, all followed Vitruvian principles. At Merida near Badajoz in Spain two storys of the *scaenae frons* have been restored and it could easily be taken for a theater located in North Africa.

Below : The architect of the amphitheater at Nimes was T. Crispius Reburrus who was also responsible for the amphitheater at nearby Arles. Twentieth in size among the 70 or so known amphitheaters it held 20,000 spectators and, like the Colosseum, it was planned so that it could easily be emptied of its audience in about five minutes.

ing official buildings, religious or secular, which project themselves. Invariably they owe their preservation in good condition to their having been utilized for other purposes, for example changed into a Christian church, or because they were incorporated in another structure and only disinterred in an enlightened age that sought their preservation. Places of entertainment, amphitheaters and theaters, seem to have survived best as upstanding monuments. Often they were in close proximity to each other, as at Arles in southern France. The closeness of the central influence of Rome, coupled with the wealth of the town and availability of suitable stone, led to many splendid amphitheaters being constructed as free-standing structures in north Italy and southern France. Where neither money nor stone were available the architect would try to utilize the natural lie of the land, as in the great amphitheater at Caerleon in South Wales, built in AD 80, the same time as the Colosseum in Rome. Great amphitheaters in stone were built in major cities such as Nîmes, Verona, Aosta, and so on, all eliptical in shape with row upon row of seats for spectators and elaborate arcading around their exteriors. Not all amphitheaters were used solely for gladiatorial combats or the savaging of helpless victims by carefully starved beasts – such entertainments were costly to stage both in money as well as in personnel. In the provinces and colonies many of the amphitheaters are attached to or close to military establishments and they would have been used a lot for parades, weapon training, tactical fighting practice and the like.

Theaters, such as those at Arles in France and Merida in Spain, are less common than amphitheaters in the western provinces. Theatrical performances began in Greece in honor of the god Dionysus; choruses would perform in a circular area before an audience seated on tiered seats, generally cut out of a hillside. From the religious beginnings sprang the whole great literature of tragedies and comedies. Rome did not, however, take over the idea of theater from the Greeks they conquered as rapidly as other cultural elements that they copied. The first permanent theater in Rome was not built until Pompey used spoils from the war with Mithradates to build one in the Campus Martius (and it was in the hall next to it that Caesar was murdered). Built of stone, it held 40,000 spectators and must have been a great novelty at the time. Two others followed swiftly, both in the Campus Martius; one was built by L Cornelius Balbus in 13 BC and the other by Augustus in the same year. Augustus dedicated it to his nephew Marcellus, who had died ten years earlier. The Roman theater was different from the Greek and where a Greek theater was taken over, as at Cyrene in North Africa, it was adapted to the Roman taste. This involved cutting across the circular dancing floor and leaving it as a segment of a circle, and usually building a tall backcloth. The Roman stage became longer and deeper. Pompeii had two theaters, a large and a small one, the latter could be covered over and was probably used more for musical presentations or readings. Ostia also had quite a substantial theater close by the Square of the Corporations. Most unusually Britain has produced evidence for five theaters in the province, but only the one at St Albans has been fully excavated and may be visited. It still retains the semicircular area before the

Left : The best preserved Roman theater in Asia Minor, at Aspendos in Turkey. The back wall of the stage building still stands to its full height of 80 feet and it has acoustics on a par with the magnificent Greek theater at Epidauros. It holds an audience of 7500 and is still used for performances.

Below : The magnificent Pont du Gard, Provence, built by Agrippa about 19 BC, carried water to Nîmes from the river Eure, a distance of about 25 miles. Its estimated daily flow was 44 million gallons, providing water for the public baths and fountains and supplies for private houses in Nîmes.

stage. At Merida, Spain, the back of the stage, the *scaena frons*, has been partly reconstructed with its columns in two tiers and is very similar, but on a smaller scale, to theaters in some of the great cities of North Africa such as Dougga and Sabratha. Although actors and scenes from plays are sometimes depicted in mosaics, generally from comedies such as those by Plautus, the actors were mainly slaves or freedmen. Paid by the magistrate, who had given the performance no doubt to enhance his own local prestige, the players were habitually despised. However, some did claim popular attention and rise to better things, such as Roscius, whose name was to become a byword in nineteenth-century England as a description for the young Shakespearian actor William Betty.

In the northern provinces of Gallia and Britannia many Roman cities are still extant and there are numerous upstanding monuments, some in much better preservation than others. Among the gems of temple architecture that survive outside Italy in this area must be counted the Maison Carée at Nîmes (ancient Nemausus). It was here that Augustus settled many of the veteran sailors who had fought for him at Actium and he had the temple erected *circa* AD 1–10. Although strictly speaking it is an Imperial Roman temple many of its features are copied from an earlier age. Built in the forum of Nemausus, it has managed to retain its open area, the sacred precinct or *temenos*,

Above: The Maison Carrée at Nîmes has served many functions since it was built in the first century BC and its continuing use has been the cause of its preservation as easily the best Roman temple surviving. It now houses the local Museum of Antiquities.

Below: Bath, *Aquae Sulis*, was a religious complex covering only 22 acres (rather than a small town) of which the focal points were the Great Bath, fed from hot natural springs deep underground, and the adjacent temple dedicated to the goddess Sulis Minerva.

around it. The high podium and the flight of approach steps are all purely classical but the enclosed *cella* (long room) for the statue of the god is typical of earlier years in the Mediterranean. The Corinthian capitals and fluted columns have close comparisons in the temple of Mars Ultor at Rome and the very fine scrollwork in the acanthus frieze reflects the similar decoration on the great Ara Pacis of Augustus in Rome. The temple is a confident provincial statement of Romanization and may be recognized as the finest example of its type north of Italy.

Not far from Nîmes stands the Pont du Gard. Inside the city the settling tank for the water it carried for the municipal services can still be seen. Whether outside Rome, in Tunisia, in Spain or here in Gaul, the aqueduct, its arches marching across the landscape, is perhaps the epitome of Roman architecture and the Roman surveyor's skill. The Pont du Gard carried water across the river Gardon, which passes through a gorge at this point. It was built by Agrippa, Augustus' son-in-law, in the first century AD. The structure throughout is of carefully squared stones set in a triple tier which is 295 yards long; it carried the water in its conduit across the river in the gorge 53 yards below. It is amazing that such a huge structure could be so harmonious in its lines. As with most ancient buildings, the secret lies in its proportions. It is based on one unit for the single arches, four units for the central arches and an overall proportion of six units for the height. There are many other aqueducts surviving throughout the Roman empire but the Pont du Gard is surely the finest in preservation and architectural presence. Another good example can be seen at Segovia in Spain but, although impressive and longer, it does not have the Pont du Gard's advantage of the splendidly picturesque river gorge crossing. At Segovia the blocks are left rough, not finished; it stretches almost 900 yards but is only about 33 yards high. Edward Gibbon was rather taken by aqueducts and wrote, 'The boldness of the enterprise, the solidity of the execution and the uses to which they were subservient, rank the aqueducts among the noblest monuments to Roman genius and power'. High praise indeed from a pen that could be extremely critical of many fields of Roman endeavor.

No matter how big or small, aqueducts throughout the empire served the basic purpose of providing the water essential for that most civilized aspect of Rome, the bath, as well as the more needful wants of drinking water and municipal sewage requirements. At Bath (Aquae Sulis) in Britain, however, the ever-bubbling hot-water springs had no need of an aqueduct, as they rose directly from deep underground. The main feature and focal point of the whole complex of baths was the Great Bath. The baths were built toward the end of the first century AD and were the *raison d'être* for the small town of about 22 acres that grew up around them. The Great Bath, originally open to the sky as we see it today, is in the center of a colonnaded hall 111 by 68

feet and itself is 80 by 40 feet and six feet deep. Subsequently the Great Bath was roofed with a huge masonry vault spanning 35 feet, supported on great masonry pillars. The steam escaped through circular openings in the roof at each end. Other baths, plunge baths, circular swimming baths and so on were all associated in the health-giving complex of the spa. Their floors were covered with massive sheets of lead up to half an inch thick. The main baths were supplied from the deep underground hot springs but certain of the other baths were heated by furnaces and some were plunge baths of cold water. The baths were part of a larger religious complex and, although they were discovered as long ago as 1755, recent excavations under the direction of Professor Barry Cunliffe are still producing much additional information and also finds, including several thousand coins which had been thrown into the bubbling waters as an offering. The great altar of the goddess Sulis Minerva has been replaced in its rightful place and new evidence has shown further details of her temple that stood beside the baths. A superb gilded bronze head of the goddess was discovered near the baths in 1727 which presumably came from a statue of her that may have stood near the entrance. Many inscribed altars have been found recording various people who had made their vows to the goddess. As well as offerings of coins, jewellery and dice have been recovered and also a small lead tablet, the 'Bath curse,' which has each word written in reverse, to make it more effective. A lover calls upon the goddess to help him dispose of the rival suitors for his girlfriend Vilbia. Such 'curse' tablets are not uncommon in shrines, often they were nailed to the walls to make sure that they remained before the deity. The hot springs, or running water, were thought to be another effective recipient. Although baths in Italy, such as those of Caracalla or Diocletian in Rome, might be far larger, the Great Bath and its attendant suites form one of the most impressive Roman monuments in western Europe, especially so in the fall months in early morning as the hot steam rises and mingles with the cold air – there is still an ancient aura about the place.

The other great upstanding monument of Roman Britain is the northern frontier, Hadrian's Wall, built in the 120s AD by an emperor noted for his incessant travelling throughout his empire. This great barrier runs from the Tyne on the east to the Solway Firth on the west – Wallsend to Bowness – a distance of just over 73 miles (80 Roman miles). As Hadrian's later biographer, Aurelius Victor, laconically wrote, 'it was built to separate the Romans from the barbarians.' Although it obviously had a defensive nature it acted mainly as a control or customs area. A series of forts averaging $7\frac{1}{2}$ miles apart ran along its length with small forts and milecastles in between. Extensive excavations have been carried out at some of the forts on the Wall, such as Housesteads and Chesters, and back-up forts such as Corbridge behind the Wall;

others still await full excavation and interpretation. In places the Wall still rises many courses high and marches, in its impressive Roman way, across hill and crag for great long stretches at a time. At the eastern end a lot of it disappeared in the military roadworks of the mid-eighteenth century AD and the modern road actually runs on top of it for some considerable distances.

A similar exercise in impressing the viewer with the majesty of Imperial Rome is the Porta Nigra at Trier in Germany. This dates to the early fourth century AD and is located in the great northern capital and mint town. Many of its features hark back to earlier, more central, Roman prototypes, especially the arched openings and the serried galleries. Unlike its earlier predecessors, however, it has a certain heaviness, particularly evident in the great flanking towers. Added to which, since it was never properly finished, its blocks have a certain rustic finish. Despite all this, it is still a magnificent example of the power of Rome standing almost on the edge of her German frontier.

While individual monuments of the northern provinces may be noticed, standing alone and ruined, on the southern boundaries of the Roman empire the situation is different. Here, along the North African coast and often far inland to the mountains, are sites of cities and towns that are almost the equivalent of Pompeii and Herculaneum. The major difference is that the North African cities were not destroyed by a major natural catastrophe, but were simply abandoned. Although many fell to the invading hordes during the later empire, they have not suffered anywhere near as much as the European monuments by the hand of man or of nature. Roman colonists were attracted to the fertile areas of North Africa as soon as Rome's old enemy Carthage was defeated after the Punic Wars. The site of Carthage itself was razed to the ground and cursed, but that did not stop eager opportunists moving into the countryside to build large country houses set

in the midst of huge estates, both of which are represented in the abundant and splendid mosaics from the area.

Modern Tunisia, the ancient heartland of Carthage, was especially favored. Perhaps the best preserved of the many Roman cities in Tunisia is Dougga (ancient Thugga). Punic in origin, it began its major expansion under Tiberius in the 30s AD. Its site is quite astounding, covering about 50 acres and with a population of around 5000 at its peak, it literally clings to the side of a mountain. Below it the slopes fall away to a tall Punic monument in the valley bottom. Although steeply set, clever use was made of the levels and the city did not lack for the necessary public buildings, the baths, theater and, not least, several temples. There is a most interesting collection of gods represented by the temple dedications which includes the usual Roman deities and the more obvious local ones such as Liber Pater (an especial patron of the emperor Septimius Severus' home town, Leptis Magna, in Libya), who is a wine god and so assimilated not only with Dionysos/

Above left: Hadrian's Wall, the northern boundary of the Empire.

Left: Trier's Porta Nigra is the largest upstanding Roman monument in northern Europe and a typical example of late Roman defenses although its arched design and heavy half-rounded towers reflect earlier styles.

Above: Dougga, the best preserved Roman city in Tunisia. Its Capitolium dominates the skyline and below is a tall second-century BC Punic mausoleum of the prince Ateban.

Below: The Capitolium at Dougga is in Corinthian style and was the gift to the city in the reign of Marcus Aurelius of a wealthy citizen.

Bacchus but also with the Punic deity Shadrach. The chief temple was the Capitolium, like many of the others a gift of some munificence by a wealthy citizen in the reign of Marcus Aurelius (built *circa* AD 166–169) and dedicated to Jupiter, Juno and Minerva. Although relatively modest in size compared with other temples, it is purely classical in concept, Corinthian and tetra-style, and owes its imposing presence (and modern photogenic situation) to its having been built on a commanding podium (it has a crypt beneath) overlooking a square that in turn drops away down the mountainside. It is undoubtedly one of the finest remaining buildings in Roman North Africa, both architecturally and in its setting. The terrain also dictated that most of the larger and grander houses were built rather in the modern idiom of 'split level' or 'town houses,' that is, the main entrance is on an upper floor with major rooms being located at a lower level down quite grand flights of stairs. It is from a number of these houses that come some of the best-known mosaic pavements in the Bardo Museum in Tunis, especially the mid-third-century representation of Ulysses tied to the mast of his ship resisting the Sirens' song.

Further southwest in Tunisia, in more open country, the town of Sufetla (modern Sbeitla) spreads a rich carpet of ruins. Its earliest inscriptions date from the reign of Vespasian, founder of the Flavian dynasty (AD 69–79). Thereafter many more appear and Sufetla features in lists of later bishoprics. A very finely decorated baptistery of the sixth century AD is still to be seen on the site with its Christian chi-rho symbols, dedication laid out in mosaic on the edge, and steps so that the initiate could walk down into it for baptism by total immersion. It has all the usual adjuncts of a

Egypt (but Egypt had a separate status, in effect being the private estate of the Emperor). Although many of the cities had prosperous earlier antecedents, especially the Punic foundations, most of the more spectacular monuments and buildings were erected in the second and early third centuries AD. The furthest west was Mauretania on the Atlantic coast. For almost half a century, equally divided over the start of the Christian era, it was ruled by Juba II, who had been given it by his friend Augustus. Juba married Cleopatra Selene, the daughter of Cleopatra VII and Mark Antony. Both had grown up as children far from their birthplaces in the household of Augustus at Rome. Juba was highly educated and a patron of the arts. From his capital at

Above left: At Sbeitla in Tunisia the Capitolium consists of three temples (presumably dedicated to Jupiter, Juno and Minerva since there are no inscriptions) that face the monumental arch of Antoninus Pius across the forum.

Right: The basilica at Volubilis, one of the finest Roman sites in Morocco. Like many of the North African cities it flourished and expanded under the Severan dynasty in the early third century AD with forum and arches being added by Septimius Severus and his son Caracalla.

Left: A well-preserved street at Djemila, Algeria. It is another of the many cities that benefitted from the African emperor Severus in the early third century AD.

civilized Roman town: a splendidly sited theater overlooking a wadi, monumental arches and a forum, all paid for by the great prosperity that the local olive industry brought to it. Its Capitolium is quite spectacular, consisting of three large temples standing side by side looking out over a paved court that is fronted with a monumental façade pierced by arches. The temples date to the mid-second century AD but their actual dedication is unknown, due to the lack of any identifying inscriptions. Probably, as at Dougga, the temples were dedicated individually to the Capitoline triad of Jupiter, Juno and Minerva. They are an imposing group in the grandeur of their disposition.

Like Tunisia, the other modern countries that were all once part of Roman North Africa have a plethora of sites, most still retaining fine monuments. To the west there is Algeria and Morocco, to the east Libya and then

Cherchel come numerous busts and statues. His second, western, capital lay at Volubilis in modern Morocco, in the mountains. Set in a fold in the mountains, the town was much enlarged and embellished under the Severan emperors. Caracalla in particular added various buildings and the usual arch, financed by heavy local taxes. He erected triumphal arches in several of the North African cities besides Volubilis; at Djemila in Algeria the Severan family buildings were much in evidence and the temple to his father Septimius Severus and the rest of the family is the normal classical Roman type approached by a long flight of steps. Although ruined and with just a few columns standing on its podium, like so many of the Roman temples of North Africa it enjoys a splendid setting with a backdrop of mountains.

To the southeast of Djemila, quite close together lay

the two cities of Lambaesis and Timgad. The former was for many years an outpost of the Third Augustan Legion and in AD 81 was made into the main garrison, being ideally and centrally situated to police the length of the province. The great forehall of the headquarters building still towers above the militarily laid out, orderly ruins. Djemila and Timgad were built as colonies for the retired veterans from the legions and their regimented grid pattern, especially evident at Timgad, bears witness to their origins. Timgad was founded in AD 100 by the emperor Trajan. On the west side, the main approach from the parent fortress Lambaesis a dozen miles away, stands an imposing triumphal arch, the so-called 'Arch of Trajan.' Virtually intact, this is one of the most complete Roman arches remaining in North Africa. The statuary that embellished it has gone, but it loses nothing for all that in its simple lines with a main arched carriageway flanked by two lesser, pedestrian archways.

The Third Augustan Legion, which was responsible for building Lambaesis, Djemila and Timgad so close together, was the only permanent legion stationed in North Africa. Once the area had been subdued there was little trouble thereafter, hence the unrivalled prosperity of the cities, reflected in their splendid buildings as rich merchants vied to present bigger and better adornments. It is known, for example, that the statues added to the triumphal arch at Timgad by Lucius Licinius Optatianus to mark his election as Perpetual Priest of the colonia cost 35,000 sesterces

(350 gold pieces, aurei), as he carefully noted in a prominent inscription. The peace and prosperity of the whole area is reflected in there only being a single legion needed to keep order on a coastline of over 3000 miles – by comparison, Britain needed at least three legions, plus auxiliaries.

Further east, in Libya, lie the two best known of the Roman cities of North Africa, Sabratha and Leptis Magna. Sabratha has its origins in a little eighth-century BC Phoenician town, a useful landfall on a long,

low, flat coast. Its initial expansion late in the first century brought it into the Roman fashion but it spread more widely in the late second century. Its greatest glory is the theater. Excavated by Italian archaeologists, they carefully restored it to the magnificent edifice it is today. The great masonry *scaena frons*, the back cloth to the stage which is preceded by a semi-circular orchestra, has been rebuilt with great care. Marble reliefs decorated the recessed front of the stage and related to the Muses, appropriately enough, as well as to many other and diverse subjects from legend and also personifications. With so magnificent a setting, its back to the sea, one can only wonder at what plays might have been produced there, what actors such as we see in the mosaics and reliefs appeared here – all must have been overshadowed by the weight, mass and magnificence of the architecture.

Below: The great apsidal-ended basilica was just one of the magnificent buildings that the emperor Septimius Severus built to honor and embellish his native city, Leptis Magna.

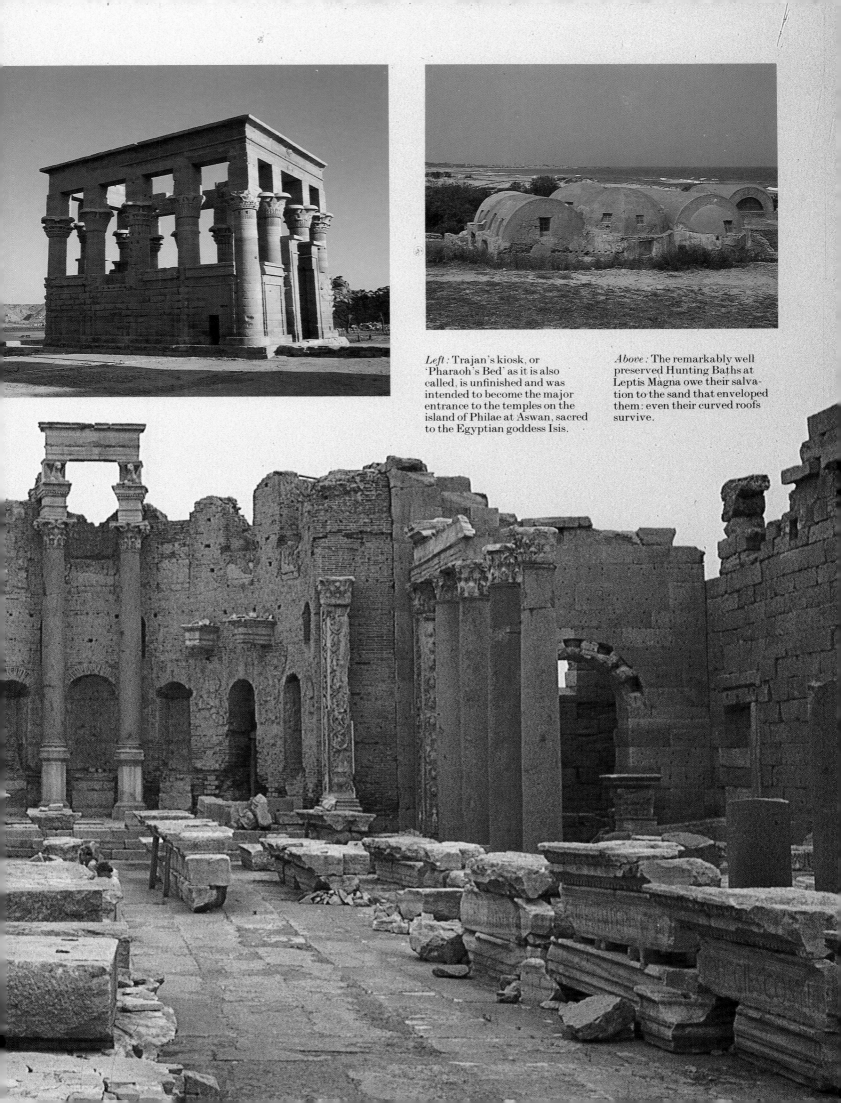

Left : Trajan's kiosk, or 'Pharaoh's Bed' as it is also called, is unfinished and was intended to become the major entrance to the temples on the island of Philae at Aswan, sacred to the Egyptian goddess Isis.

Above : The remarkably well preserved Hunting Baths at Leptis Magna owe their salvation to the sand that enveloped them : even their curved roofs survive.

Leptis Magna, 120 miles further east, closer to Egypt, began life as a small and safe anchorage on a very long and difficult coast in Carthaginian or Phoenician times. It was a convenient place at the mouth of the wadi Lebda on the long haul from the Levant to Spain. Naturally its size increased with its prosperity. Its large market place, which has quite an unusual design, was the gift of a wealthy citizen, Annobal Rufus, in 9–8 BC. His name is half Phoenician and this is found to be the case with many of the names recorded in inscriptions in the city – the old wealthy families lived on and accepted a Roman veneer. The same philanthropist presented the city with its theater in AD 1–2 and inscriptions still extant, carved in Latin and Neo-Punic above two of the entrances to the orchestra, record his munificence. Close by a temple dedicated to the Deified Emperors was built in AD 43 by Iddibal Tapapius, a relative of Annobal Rufus. Obviously a lot of the local wealth was held by the family and they were not miserly in their provision of civic amenities.

Among the many fine buildings and ruins that delight the eye and form such a magnificent vista at Leptis are the 'Hunting Baths' down by the seashore. Built in the second century AD they were covered over by wind-blown sand and preserved virtually intact beneath the dunes. Their domes are mostly original with only slight areas of restoration or repair. They are unique in the Roman Empire in their preservation. The future emperor Septimius Severus (AD 193–211) was born at Leptis Magna and it is not to be wondered that when he had attained the 'purple' a number of North Africans appear in high positions of trust under him and that Leptis enters upon a golden age of building. Among the many buildings is an addition to the city's arches, a magnificently decorated four-way example with fine sculptures of the emperor and his family (it is said that he was quite ashamed of his sister's strong Punic accent when she spoke Latin). The major scene in relief records Septimius' visit to the city in AD 203. In all there were four major relief panels above the cornice, and 24 smaller sculpted panels vertically in threes on the four inner faces of the piers. The smaller panels have suffered heavily but the upper panels have fared better (except in the case of Geta, who was murdered by his brother Caracalla after Septimius' death and whose image suffered – the sawn-off head of Geta's statue was found buried beside the arch). Such was the enthusiasm of the citizens to embellish their town in the Severan period (end of the second and early third century AD) that they also added great quays and warehouses. These partly dammed the wadi Lebda, built up silt and the harbors were soon rendered useless. The city began to decline, imperial buildings were left unfinished and it shrank back to a comparatively tiny area around the old forum and the mouth of the wadi.

Egypt, although it became part of the Roman Empire when Octavian entered Alexandria on 1 August 30 BC, hardly noticed the advent of Rome. It enjoyed a curious and privileged position in relation to the other provinces, remaining virtually the private estate of the emperor. The old ways continued much as before but now, instead of Egyptian pharaohs appearing on the wall reliefs of the temples (or Graeco-Egyptian under the Ptolemies), the emperors were represented in the guise and dress of pharaoh. Many of the great Ptolemaic temples such as Dendera, Edfu and Kom Ombo had additions made in the names of various emperors; the hypostyle hall at Esna copied the plan of earlier Dendera, but with Roman emperors represented and their names in the royal cartouches. The very epitome of Egyptian building skills (aside from the pyramids of Giza) is, strangely, a building of Roman date in Egyptian style. This is the so-called 'Pharaoh's Bed,' Trajan's kiosk, built on Philae, the island sacred to the goddess Isis at Aswan deep in southern Egypt. Many Roman emperors added small temples and gateways to the religious complex on the island but Trajan's (AD 96–117) addition, although it has a certain grace today, was never actually completed. The sistrum capitals intended to cap the floral capitals were never carved, nor were the majority of the intermediate screens between the side wall columns. The building was actually intended to be a formal entry from the river into the temple and today it is its sheer simplicity because of being unfinished, coupled with its massive design, that appeals, making it the major architectural treasure of Roman Egypt.

The eastern Roman provinces, which largely came under Rome's jurisdiction after Pompey the Great's conquests in 64 BC, were a rather tentative coalition between East and West, Greece and Rome. The 'oriental' element was always present and Rome, as it often did, realized that it was best to adapt and accept the *status quo* rather than endeavor to change everything into true Roman ways and foundations. This is especially evident in what is now the Lebanon. There are many ruins of Roman temples and buildings throughout the Levant but the area that overshadows them all is Baalbek with its great sanctuary begun in the early first century AD and finished in the mid-third. Earlier sanctuaries on the site beneath the Roman structures go back as far as the sixth century BC. The temple of Jupiter dominates the site, its height enhanced by its 44-foot high podium above which tower 65-foot columns – the total height from the court to the gable was 130 feet and the temple measured 158 by 259 feet. While the proportions are essentially those of a classical Roman temple, many elements of eastern Hellenistic decoration can be seen in the sculptural decoration. The nearby temple of Bacchus (115 by 217 feet) would be deemed large were it not for its massive neighbor. Its decoration is quite elaborate and in both temples their size is coupled with architectural conceits to produce illusions of even greater size. By contrast the third temple, built in the third century and dedicated to Venus, is quite elegant. It has a circular *cella*, as

Below : The huge columns of the temple of Jupiter at Baalbek stand on a plinth and quite overshadow the temple of Bacchus behind, which itself is of immense size.

Above : One of the best preserved and certainly largest and most complete Roman temples in the eastern Empire, the temple of Bacchus at Baalbek, Lebanon, dwarfs mere mortals passing by.

against the great oblong ones of its companions across the street, an outer colonnade that stands on a tall, scalloped podium and a shallow stone domed roof. As usual, it is approached by a flight of steps leading to a square pronaos that fronts the *cella*. While it betrays, like the others, elements of Hellenistic architectural origins it has at the same time many elements that form the basis of the European Baroque still some centuries ahead.

As in the North African province, conditions, both economic and natural, have been instrumental in preserving numerous cities of the eastern Roman empire. One of the best surviving is Jerash (ancient Gerasa) in Jordan. At first little touched by the coming of Rome, it began to expand in the later first century but the vast spread of ruins and upstanding buildings we see today were largely built between AD 50–200. The street plan was enlarged, its polygonal shape surrounded by a strong circuit of walls and appropriate gates and its two major streets that crossed the town were carried on bridges over the river Chrysorhoas that bisected the town. In AD 106 it became part of the province of Arabia (recently annexed to Rome). Under the emperors Trajan, Hadrian and Antoninus Pius new gates, temples, theaters and baths were added. The main temple was to Artemis, standing within its rectangular temenos and having a great monumental approach, still largely upstanding, that guarded a long flight of approach steps. Despite the grandeur of the buildings remaining it is the oval piazza with its graceful line of columns close by the South Theater that catches the eye more today.

In Asia Minor great cities also abounded, many ruins can still be examined but it is Ephesus that claims most attention. Essentially it was a Hellenistic city, the city of Lysimachos, Alexander's trusted general and old friend. It was a city dedicated to the goddess Artemis, her temple outside the walls had its foundation in antiquity and was listed as one of the Seven Wonders of the Ancient World. Parts of the city and its additional Roman buildings are still being excavated by Austrian archaeologists. Its main street is lined with inscriptions and statues and among the buildings the little temple of Hadrian is a minor gem, quite modest but of very pleasing proportions. At the bottom of the street stands, by contrast, an imposing reconstruction of the Library of Celsus, its façade having been painstakingly worked out. It was built between AD 117–120 in the reign of Trajan to honor Caius Julius Celsus Polemaeanus, a citizen of Ephesus distinguished both by his wealth and the fact that he had been consul in Rome. In recognition of the latter he was accorded the highly unusual privilege of being buried within the city limits (contrary to normal Roman Law) in a vault beneath the apse of the Library. His pious son and grandson completed the building. Other buildings of note at Ephesus are the two theaters, the larger, built into the hillside just beyond the Library, holding an audience of about 24,000.

Other unusual tombs, but not quite like the Library of Celsus, may be found throughout the empire. One of the strangest stands in Rome itself, just outside the Porta San Paolo, the pyramid of Gaius Cestius, praetor, tribune and member of the college of the Septemviri Epulones (who were in charge of solemn banquets). Built of brick-faced marble, its rather steeply angled sides rise to 121 feet from a 100-foot square base. It is built across the line of the city wall and part of it now stands in the Protestant Cemetery where Keats is buried. Gaius Cestius died in 43 BC and an inscription records that the monument was erected in 330 days. Why he should have chosen such a curious and idiosyncratic shape for his tomb is not known and, at the date when he died, Egypt had not yet been brought into the Roman empire. The more usual shapes of tombs were the great drum structures like the mausoleum of Augustus where the ashes of most of the immediate Imperial family were interred. It has a diameter of 292 feet and was originally covered with a mound of earth 145 feet high planted with trees and topped by a statue of Augustus. It has its origins in Etruscan architecture and it was one of the most sacred monuments of ancient Rome. The well-known contemporary and similar circular tomb of Caecilia Metalla just outside Rome on the Appian Way only has a diameter of 65½ feet but is still very imposing.

Top right: The grandiose sweep of the colonnade at Jerash, Jordan.

Top: At Ephesus the library of Celsus built under Hadrian is one of the most splendid buildings of a magnificent city. The façade is a meticulous restoration.

Right: Why the praetor and tribune Gaius Cestius chose such an unusual shape as a pyramid for his tomb is not known. Built in 43 BC, it anticipated Octavian's Egyptian conquests by 13 years. Beyond it is the Porta San

Paolo, the outer face of which was rebuilt by Honorius in AD 402.

Above: On the left bank of the Tiber the great drum-shape of the Castel Sant 'Angelo was originally the mausoleum of Hadrian and of subsequent Roman emperors down to Caracalla, who was murdered in 217. In the second century it had a tumulus of earth on top that was planted with cypress trees, like the earlier mausoleum of Augustus nearby on the east bank.

Another great circular tomb, but set on a square podium, is the Castel Sant' Angelo, the mausoleum of Hadrian finished by his successor Antoninus Pius in AD 139, the year after Hadrian's death. This consists of a round tower 210 feet in diameter on a 275-foot square base. The ashes of all the Roman emperors from Hadrian to Caracalla (died AD 217) were buried here but, like so

many of the other great Roman tombs, especially the two first mentioned, it was turned into a fortress in the Middle Ages. It was subsequently used as a barracks, then a prison, down until 1901 when it was reprieved and inaugurated in 1925 as a fine military and artistic museum.

Funerary monuments abound throughout the Roman empire, mostly rather battered relics that have long since been robbed of their sculptured reliefs or were just fabric for reuse as building materials in a later age. Roman Law decreed that burials should be outside the confines of the town and the monuments tend to be found lining the major roads from the town or city gate, such as one finds along the Appian Way southward from the Porta Sebastiano of Rome (where the catacombs also were excavated deep underground). Some monuments have survived in various parts of the empire that are good examples of their type. At St Rémy (ancient Glanum) in Provence, France, the monument of the Julii, dating from the late Republic stands close beside a triumphal arch of *circa* AD 10–20. The Julii were a prosperous local family of influence, as shown by their splendid monument which rises from a heavy podium that has four large relief panels showing active battles and hunts and, above that, a four-way arch surmounted by a quite graceful circular cupola of 12 Corinthian columns which shelters the statues of the

Above: At Tuna el-Gebel in middle Egypt the fine wind-blown sand buried the cemetery and thus preserved its large stone-built tombs virtually intact. The solidity of the structures reflects the Roman settlers adoption of the ancient Egyptian idea of the tomb being a 'house of Eternity.'

deceased. Nearly 60 feet high, this funerary monument on the outposts of empire is far superior to any similar examples to be found in Italy. Further north, in Germany at Igel outside Trier, the great northern capital, another tall tower-tomb stands which dates from the early third century AD. It is the monument to the Secundinii, erected by two sons to commemorate their parents, 'parentibus defunctis,' and themselves, 'sibi vivi,' as we learn from the inscriptions on it. This still stands to its original height of about 70 feet, built of sandstone rising from a four-stepped base and with interesting reliefs indicating that the source of the family's wealth lay in cloth-making. The members of the family commemorated were probably buried in graves nearby.

Of a totally different design and located in the later capital of Ravenna is the delightful mausoleum of Galla Placidia, sister of the emperor Honorius, built *circa* AD 425, although she did not die until 450. It is a small cruciform building with a plain exterior simply decorated with pilasters and blind arcades. Its honey-colored alabaster windows let soft light into the interior which is resplendent with mosaics, largely featuring blue and with Christian iconography as their major subjects.

On the southern boundaries of the empire, along the North African coast, individual tomb monuments to be found are mostly dilapidated but at Tuna el-Gebel in middle Egypt, close by the ancient Hermopolis Magna, an extensive cemetery stands in the desert. Extending from the late New Kingdom into Roman times, the blown sand has preserved the monuments virtually intact. Those of the Roman period are tomb-houses, carefully constructed and far better than the houses that the living would have had in the area. To these, at the appropriate festivals, the relatives would come to eat a meal with the deceased and celebrate them – much the same thing still occurs in the Muslim religion when on certain days the cemeteries are alive with family reunions.

Thousands of Roman buildings are still extant throughout the length and breadth of the Roman empire in varying stages of preservation. Some are still very obviously great treasures of building, others perhaps more like smaller gems that have to be noticed to be appreciated. All, however, betoken the master builders of Rome.

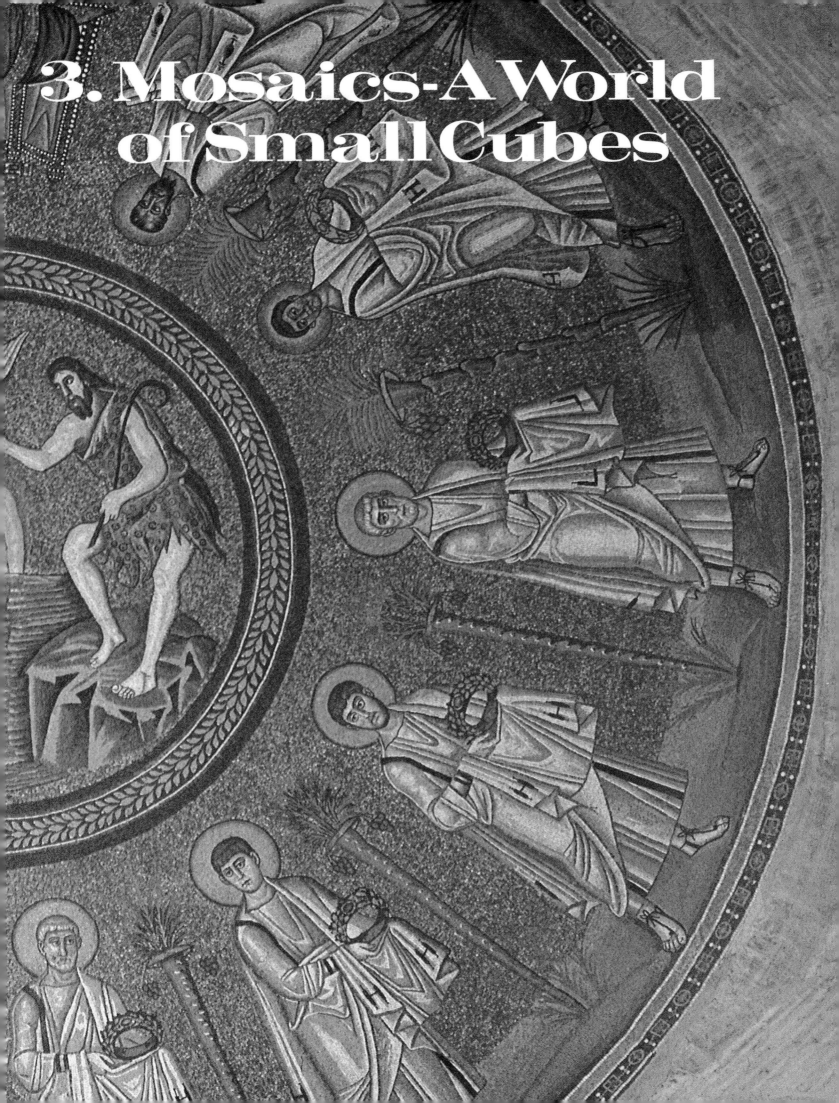

3. Mosaics–A World of Small Cubes

To many, brightly colored mosaics, generally thought of as being laid on floors, are the one thing that they remember when they are seen *in situ* on ancient sites or displayed in museums. In museums they are rarely displayed in their original manner but tend to be placed on walls. This often works quite well and certainly the lower halves of figured mosaics can be seen better, but two things are missed: first, the parts higher up on the wall tend to be lost in the distance or distorted by the viewpoint; second, floor mosaics in the Roman world were generally laid with a very specific viewpoint from which they should be seen. They were, in a way, the ancient world's version of the modern fitted carpet. This is not to say that all mosaics are therefore floor mosaics, they are not. Mosaics were used to decorate walls and vaults and no one surely can fail to respond to the gloriously dazzling roof mosaics, invariably heavy with blue and gold, that are among the splendors of so many Byzantine churches in Italy, as at Ravenna, and in Greece with its thousands of monasteries and churches.

The art of floor mosaic probably began in Asia Minor, the first mosaic floors being made up simply of selected water-worn pebbles. Such a geometrically decorated floor has been found at Gordion (home of the famous 'Gordian Knot' of Alexander the Great legend) and dated to the eighth/seventh centuries BC. At the Macedonian royal capital of Pella in northern Greece there is a series of animated pebble mosaics that includes scenes from a lion hunt, the whole illustrated very much in the heroic Alexander tradition. These date to the later fourth century BC, and similar simply constructed mosaics are also found at the Greek city of Olynthos. At both these sites the mosaics show great artistic merit and accomplishment. Such floors embellished the major public rooms of private houses, the dining or banqueting room, and often had central medallions that featured scenes from classical legends. It can be interesting to pursue some of these motifs down the centuries and often across wide geographical areas. For example, a pebble mosaic at Olynthos shows the hero Bellerophon riding his famous winged horse Pegasus and attacking the fabulous chimaera. Over the course of the next six or more centuries the same subject can be found represented as far away from Olynthos as Roman Britain in a mosaic still *in situ* in the villa at Lullingstone, Kent, and on another from Hinton St Mary, Dorset (now in the British Museum). On the latter this pagan motif is associated with a representation of Christ. Both these mosaics date from the fourth century AD.

Most of the early mosaics relied a lot on producing their effect by contrasting light and dark stones, essentially a reflection of the techniques found on Greek painted pottery known as black-figure and red-figure where, as the names imply, the major figures are in the named color on a contrasting background. From such cities already mentioned, and places like the free port of the island of Delos with its magnificent houses and figured mosaics, the art of mosaic moved from the Hellenistic world to the world of Rome, to its private houses as well as to its public buildings and temples. Delicately figured mosaics were found in the pronaos of the great temple of Zeus at Olympia (itself one of the Seven Wonders of the Ancient World) and in the late Republic mosaics are introduced into the great temples such as that of Fortuna at Palestrina, just north of Rome.

First, one should have some idea of the techniques involved to be able to appreciate more fully the skill of the craftsmen producing these often vast areas of illustration in tiny cubes of stone. Quite early on it was realized that greater accuracy of detail could be obtained by cutting the stones and not simply relying on producing the effect or detail by a finely graduated sequence of water-worn pebbles. Perhaps a single small stone could be cut to give the effect of an eye in a profile portrait; the addition of further, more finely cut stones, could enhance the representation and make it more lifelike. These small cut stones are called *tesserae* and their use opened up whole new aspects of the mosaicist's art. At first, most *tesserae* were cut from whatever happened to be the locally occurring stones, supplemented perhaps by the use of fragments of terracotta, pottery and glass. Gradually, as the techniques were better mastered and as patrons wanted bigger and better representations, both as to subject and color, special stones were imported from different parts of the empire. Marble is one of the most obvious choices, with its varying textures and shades of coloring. The small cubes were probably brought down to their rough size by using small portable iron anvils that could be socketed into a block of wood. Refinements in shaping were carried out by the use of pincers; this technique is still used, as in the restoration of the Orpheus Mosaic at Littlecote in England.

Having acquired the requisite quantities of raw material, the next step was to have a suitable bed prepared for the mosaic. We know exactly how this should be done because it was described by the famous Roman architect and engineer Marcus Vitruvius Pollio who lived in the late first century BC in the reign of Augustus and who wrote his famous *De architectura* in ten volumes. In Book VII are the instructions for laying floors: the ground must first be tested to check that everywhere is solid with no old walls or hidden ditches under the proposed site; a firm base is next constructed 'of stones not smaller than can fill the hand'; next, the broken stone, if it is new, is mixed three parts to one of lime, if it is old then five parts to two. 'Next, lay the mixture of broken stone, bring on your gangs, and beat it again and again with wooden beetles into a solid mass, and let it be not less than three quarters of a foot in thickness when the beating is finished.' On top of this a six-inch layer of crushed tile and mortar is

spread and the resultant surface is ready to receive its pavement. The solidity of the base is strongly stressed and nowadays it can be seen where the Roman builder did not strictly follow Vitruvius' instructions; pavements laid over hidden ditches develop switchback tendencies, others laid above a hypocaust heating system on too shallow a foundation crack with the heat and tumble down among the supporting piers of the hypocaust.

The next problem is how to lay the proposed mosaic on the prepared surface. Basic guidelines can be scored or painted on the surface, indicating the broad features of the design to come. The actual laying of the mosaic can be done in one of three ways. The first, and most obvious, is the direct method of laying a bedding of mortar and building up the pattern by placing the tesserae directly onto it while it was still moist. When finished it would be pressed into position and a semi-liquid solution of mortar forced in between the pieces to give a more secure bonding. In the second, indirect, method the pattern or design was laid out first, probably in sections if it was a big mosaic, in large trays of sand. Then something such as a strong piece of linen was pasted or glued onto the tesserae. When it was dry and set the sections could be moved into their appropriate positions on the prepared bedding mortar. Once all was firmly set the linen could be soaked off with water. A third method, the reverse method, was similar to the second except that the tesserae were glued face down on a colored cartoon on the linen. Each section was laid by being lifted from the workshops, turned upside down on the site and placed in position and the cartoon 'backing' soaked off.

Probably the last two methods described were the most frequently used since they were quite effective. Work could be done 'off site' and then just moved and laid as appropriate. Stereotype decorations, such as the frequently found edging of guilloche patterns, could be 'prefabricated' and kept in stock. It is in this prefabri-

cation that human error can creep in and really bring home to us the essential essence of ancient Rome when perhaps a frame is found to be too small for the main motif, or sections of pattern do not join exactly as they should and a little 'adjustment' had to be made. Often the central motifs would be the work of the senior craftsmen and apprentices would produce the repetitive edge designs or plain backgrounds.

The principal motifs would be selected by the owner of the villa, or some kind of committee presumably for large public buildings. Study of mosaics over the years now indicates that not only were there individual identifiable workshops and styles but also pattern books which must have been shown to the customer. Many subjects occur time and again over the centuries, especially those from popular myths such as Bellerophon, Pegasus and the chimaera already mentioned, or from epic narratives such as the Odyssey, where Ulysses and the sirens was a favorite – it is known from Tor Marancia, Italy, in black and white mosaic (now in the Vatican) and away in North Africa in the splendidly polychrome mosaic from Dougga (now in the Bardo Museum, Tunis), as well as many other sites. Within an area there is a tendency for mosaics to be 'recognizable' as from that area and there are times when suddenly it becomes apparent that a pattern has been imported. Mosaics such as the lion and stag at St Albans, and Aeneas and Dido from Low Ham, both show their North African origins; the curious Abraxes figure at Bignor on the Isle of Wight indicates both the villa owner's personal indication and taste as well as something more appropriate to the eastern Mediterranean. Three such examples alone taken from Roman Britain indicate well how patterns, and the people who composed and laid them, could move about the Roman empire.

Literally thousands of mosaics survive from ancient Rome and from virtually every part of her vast empire. Although the basic techniques were the same, the

content often similar in as much as themes from myth, religion or literature appear, some areas are richer than others because of simple economic factors and, not least, the hazards of survival.

In view of the often glorious colors of the later mosaics (and a high proportion of the polychrome mosaics often seen illustrated date from the very late third and fourth centuries AD), the relatively plain black and white mosaics that were a feature of the late years of the Republic and the early years of Imperial Rome, are often overlooked. They should not be because they often show a vivacity and skill of rendition that is lacking in later mosaics and which is obscured by the latter's use of bright color. The black-and-white style properly emerges around 20 BC and is best represented in the second and early third centuries AD. Ostia, the ancient port of Rome, has produced over a thousand mosaics in this style and here many of them can still be seen as they were laid, a constant surprise and delight on the site as you walk round a corner to be confronted by some strange beast, or step on one of the many viewing areas to look down on a vast expanse of lively animation. It must not be expected that all mosaics are masterpieces, many are simply rather mundane little pieces of work that served an essentially utilitarian purpose. Such is the case with the series of

black-and-white mosaics at Ostia that were laid in the row of small offices built around three sides of the Piazza delle Corporazioni (The Square of the Corporations, or Guilds) in the second century AD. Here there were 70 small offices ranging from workers' guilds to foreign mercantile interests. Preserved in the mosaic floors are the names of many of them, telling us where they traded from and with representations appropriate to their trade or products. As may be expected, many ships and varieties of animals are represented, as are fish, men loading amphorae onto merchantmen and several different versions of lighthouses (all stemming in their plan from the great Pharos, the lighthouse, of Alexandria, one of the Seven Wonders of the Ancient World that was still in effective use at that time).

By contrast, the black-and-white mosaic pavements in the Baths of Neptune are alive and fantastically animated. These were completed in AD 139 and are in the so-called 'figural' style; they are perhaps the finest and best-known mosaics of their type. The whole of the floor of the great entrance hall of the baths is filled with Neptune driving four lively sea horses surrounded by tritons, mermen with crab's claws in their hair, sea panthers, Nereids riding on the backs of sea horses, cupids riding dolphins (rather like the earlier, famous examples on Delos), dolphins sporting alone and, within all this fantastic maritime activity, two male figures are shown swimming to the left below Neptune's sea horses. Such is the skill and virtuosity of this mosaic that the artist who created it has been dubbed 'The Master of the Neptune mosaic.' In the adjoining room on the south another mosaic of smaller size shows Amphitrite reclining on the back of a sea horse preceded by a flying Hymen holding a torch and flanked by mermen with cymbals. She is being led to her wedding with Neptune. The mosaic on the north side of the Neptune mosaic features the sea monster Scylla and is cleverly com-

ΓΝωΘΙ CAYTON

Above: The reclining skeleton and its Greek inscription ('Know thyself'). Museo Nazionale, Rome.

Right: An amusing mosaic from Pompeii shows a skeleton firmly grasping a wine jug in each hand. Museuo Nazionale, Naples.

posed to give an impression of her all-pervading presence with her sea creatures in a space that appears to be limitless by not having any confines to the mosaic save the walls themselves. The three mosaics together form the largest group of these figural black-and-white mosaics that can be seen in their original architectural setting.

At Ostia the largest collection of black-and-white figural mosaics can be seen *in situ* and they extend down into the Severan period of the early third century. Early ones at Pompeii are in some instances better known, especially the ferocious guard dog on its chain with its inscription in mosaic 'Cave Canem' (Beware of the dog!) at the entrance to the house of the Tragic Poet.

Some mosaic subjects are very curious to our eyes as a choice of ornament. The great mosaicist Sosos of Pergamon is said to have invented many specific motifs and one of them that became popular in ancient Rome was the *asaraton* mosaic (the unswept floor). A particularly fine example from Rome shows the scatter of left overs from a banquet; fish skeletons still with their heads on, crabs' legs, whelk shells, wishbones, cherry stones and so on – all very accurately represented. Other semihumorous subjects occur, like the skeleton on a mosaic from Pompeii carrying a wine jug in each hand. Another skeleton, from Rome, this time reclining on what almost appears to be a bed of nails, has the admonition in Greek ΓΝΩΘΙ CAYTON – Know Thyself! An illustration of the degree of superstition that was always present in Roman life is a mosaic from

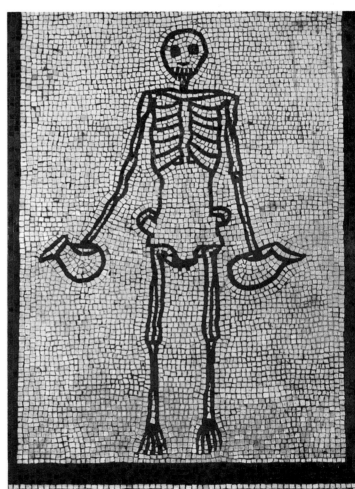

Right: Nilotic scenes, especially with often weird looking crocodiles and hippopotami, were quite widespread among Roman mosaics and continued to be reproduced into the late Empire even in Christian churches. Undoubtedly the greatest of this type of mosaic is that at Palestrina outside Rome which is alive with all manner of strange animals, pygmies, buildings and boats as it depicts the annual inundation of the Nile.

the Basilica Hiliarana in Rome. The building identifies its name by giving it in the mosaic inscription at the entrance. It was built about AD 150 by a rich pearl merchant, M Poblicius Hilarus and was sacred to the cults of the Magna Mater (the Great Mother, Cybele) and Attis. In the vestibule, at the foot of a flight of 12 steps and under the mosaic inscription in its ansate plaque, the evil eye is represented with an owl perched on it and a spear piercing it through. Including the owl, it is being attacked by a group of nine (itself a magical number, being 3 by 3) animals and birds that include a leopard, bull, crow and a scorpion.

One of the earliest and largest Roman mosaics was laid in the great temple of Fortuna at Palestrina (ancient Praeneste). The temple was so large – laid out on a series of terraces as it was rebuilt under the dictator Sulla in 82 BC – that the whole of the later medieval town was enclosed within it. It covered an area of about 80 acres which gives a good indication of its importance and standing as a religious center. The great mosaic (variously known as the Palestrina, Praeneste, or Barberini mosaic) presents a bird's eye view of Egypt at the inundation of the Nile in quite

Above: The aversion of the Evil Eye, omens and portents were a potent part of Roman life and this mosaic from the Basilica Hilariani shows an interesting collection of birds and animals attacking the evil eye, which is pierced by a spear. Museo dei Conservatori, Rome.

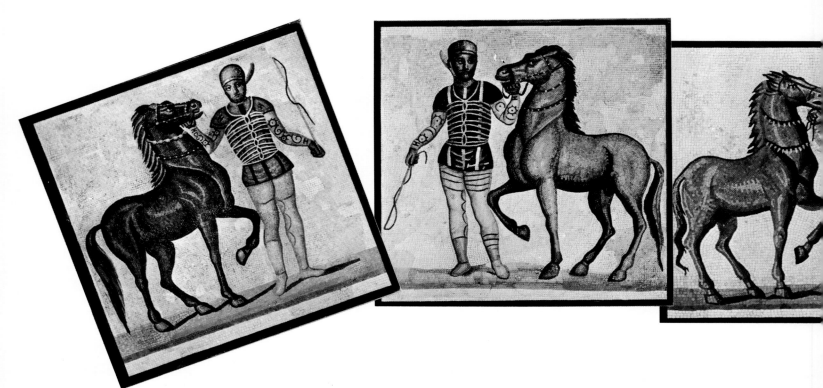

brilliant colors. It runs from the source of the Nile among the mountains of Ethiopia (Abyssinia) at the top to the broad Delta at the bottom. The detail in it is incredible even if much of it is fantastic. Various temples are shown, some in proper Egyptian style with great pylon towers before them with statues against them, others are in the Graeco-Hellenistic style of architecture. At the other end of the architectural scale are the papyrus-built shelters of the Arab peasants in the fields. The aquatic animals, especially the crocodiles and hippopotami, are well 'drawn' but some of the other animals thought to lurk in Central Africa are very odd, even though they are amusingly labelled in Greek. At the bottom there is quite a detailed representation of a colonnaded building with a 'sun shade' (?) drawn to one side to reveal a group of soldiers and a priestess.

This presumably is supposed to be in Alexandria and may represent the Serapeum, the temple of Serapis that was part of a large religious complex which also included the world-famous library.

The Palestrina mosaic is the largest and best known of these so-called 'Nilotic' mosaics that became very popular. A number of them, naturally, occur appropriately enough in religious contexts allied with the cult of the great Egyptian goddess Isis.

There are so many fine mosaics which have survived, either *in situ* or, more commonly, removed to museums for preservation, that it is difficult to make an overall assessment. They can be examined chronologically, by geographical area or by their actual content and representations. Perhaps a general approach along the latter lines is best.

based on the picture known to have been painted by Philoxenos in 318 BC. Both the house and mosaic are of the late-Hellenistic style rather than Roman but are interesting in that they should have retained this unaltered into the first century AD.

Particularly favored as mosaic representation were scenes of entertainment, especially relating to the amphitheater or circus. Political factions in Rome identified themselves by association with the four colors of the charioteers in the circus, notably the blues or the greens. Riots were not unknown when a color not favored by the masses and the current political party won. Typical of such favorite charioteers are those in a mosaic from the Villa dei Settimii where four charioteers are seen in the appropriate colors wearing their protective leather caps and leather chest bands, each holding a high-spirited horse. Representations of the actual racing commonly occur on reliefs rather than in mosaics.

Gladiatorial combats feature more than racing in the mosaics and there is a definite tendency for them to be more popular in Roman North Africa than elsewhere in the empire. Many examples are known from that province, most of fairly high quality in their rendition of ferocious scenes of attack. The roar of the crowd in the amphitheater, the blood lust that it could rouse, was all translated into mosaic where the provision of a mosaic so detailed as to include even the gladiators' names must have been a very great expense for a villa owner obviously besotted with the arena. Many gladiators were foreign prisoners forced to fight each other with their own weapons and in their own style. Mosaics often show in their detail the various types of gladiator that would be produced in the famous train-

Pompeii and Herculaneum, by virtue of their rapid destruction, have preserved a fine selection of mosaics that have the advantage, archaeologically, of at least having a terminal date in AD 79, even if some of the earlier dating is open to discussion. Perhaps the most famous mosaic from the area (now in the Museo Nazionale, Naples) is the 'Issus' mosaic found in the House of the Faun at Pompeii. Strictly speaking this great pictorial mosaic is in the Hellenistic tradition. 'Painted' in only four colors (black, white, red and yellow), it shows the personal encounter between Alexander the Great and the Persian king Darius at the battle of Issus in 333 BC. The mosaic was probably

ing schools such as at Capua. The heavily armored type were known as Samnites; they were magnificently equipped with oblong shields (*scutum*); a heavy vizored helmet often with a huge metal crest (*galea*); a greave or shin guard (*ocrea*) normally on the left leg (the one advanced in combat), and a stabbing sword (*gladius*). These were the earliest type of gladiator in Rome. Other main types were the Thracians, armed with a small square or round shield, a curved scimitar and a pair of leg greaves; the *retiarius* had a throwing net, a long trident or tunny-fish harpoon and a dagger. There were many variations on the standard equipment ranging across the empire. On a mosaic from a rich villa at Zliten (now in the Tripoli Museum) the outer border shows both gladiatorial combats and wild beast displays in great detail. In one corner (repeated later) there is a four-piece orchestra consisting of two men with curved trumpets or horns (*cornu*), another with a long straight trumpet (*tuba*) and, most unusual, a water organ (*organum*) which is being played by a woman. Just behind them a bier ominously waits for the losers from the fighting that extends away in front. Various types of gladiator are represented, as well as helpless victims like the man tied to a pole on a small go-cart that is being propelled forward to be savaged by a panther; his companion in adversity already has the beast upon him. Elsewhere a bear and a bull are tied together by a chain in a fight to the death and another helpless prisoner is held by his back hair and thrust toward a leaping lion, his captor wielding a long whip for his own protection.

While all these detailed and grisly scenes can appear in a mosaic that has obviously been specially and expensively commissioned, it is curious that another side of the Roman character can be observed within the same subject. At Bignor, Sussex, gladiators are also represented, but this time they are amusing little fellows – cupids training as gladiators in a charming series of vignettes – that are associated with a pleasing representation of a bust of Venus in a lunette above them. These gladiator mosaics in such different style and feeling, carried out several thousand miles apart from one end of the Roman empire to another, both date to the fourth century AD.

That most of such spectacles were put on for public amusement at private expense is best evidenced by a

Below left: The outer frieze or border of a mosaic from Zliten, Libya, with its savage details of bestiality is a monument to both the skill of the mosaicist and to Roman bad taste. Tripoli Museum, Libya.

Left: A detail from a third-century mosaic in the villa at Bignor in Sussex shows another aspect of the Roman character when gladiators could be humorously shown as cupids training under their managers.

Right: Most unusually, this third-century mosaic from a large house at Moknine, Tunisia, shows not only the *bestiarii* actively killing a group of leopards but names both them and the animals. In the center, but totally unassociated with the surrounding activity, a young man carries a tray laden with bags of money. Sousse Museum, Tunisia.

Below: The Great Hunt is a favorite motif in many large villas. One of the best representations is in the Imperial villa at Piazza Armerina, Sicily, dating to the late third/early fourth century AD.

61

mosaic from Smirat in Tunisia (now in the Sousse Museum). This shows a very lively scene of a group of *venatores* and leopards, all of whom are named in the inscriptions. The action is extremely realistic but the scene conflates two events by the representation of a boy in the center carrying a tray upon which are four bags of money. On either side of him are two very long inscriptions. That on the left records the appeal made to the audience at the end of the contest to contribute and pay the price of 500 denarii per leopard. The longer inscription on the right records the audience's acclamation when one Magirius takes it upon himself not only to pay the sum per leopard asked but, as the little symbol on each money bag indicates, he doubles it to 1000 denarii per leopard. Magirius himself is represented at the top right of the mosaic by the remnants of a richly dressed standing figure, identified by inscription, who stands beside the god Dionysus under whose nominal patronage, no doubt, the display was staged. Such a record in a mosaic is most unusual, it is more expected to be found in an inscription in a public place. Here, Magirius obviously preferred to record the event and his munificence in his own house, specifying exactly the content of the mosaic, as a permanent illustration for himself and his guests. The event depicted must have taken place at somewhere such as nearby Thysdrus since Smirat was quite a small place and had no amphitheater. Magirius was probably the owner of a large estate in the area and his house the focal point.

Sometimes the animals did get a rest and a mosaic from the same broad area, from El Djem, shows the *venatores* at a banquet, which gives the bulls the opportunity to sleep silently, as the Latin caption points out.

The capturing of the wild animals for shows in North Africa and in Italy itself was a profitable and also extremely hazardous business. At the great villa at Piazza Armerina in Sicily a whole range of the numerous mosaics found there relate to this trade and show the hunt in detail. Stylistically the mosaics are close to the North African ones, showing similar scenes of the hunt. Not all the animals hunted are the large savage beasts for the circus, one detail shows a mounted huntsman thrusting down with his spear at a rabbit crouched in a small thicket. Other scenes show the aftermath of capture, the loading onto the ships for the Italian ports of crated animals, others are slung on poles or, such as an elephant, being guided up the gang plank. Nearby a rather contemplative, richly dressed figure wearing a cylindrical cap, typical of the Tetrarchic period at the end of the third century AD, is probably the owner of the villa, the emperor Maximianus who is known to have retired to Sicily in AD 305 when he and his colleague Diocletian abdicated.

There are a host of other mosaics in this villa, many of them mythological in content, such as Ulysses and the Cyclops Polyphemus; Hesion and Endymion;

Above: It is thought that the melancholy looking figure wearing a low round hat and leaning on a staff in the mosaic at Piazza Armerina represents the owner who may have been the emperor Maximianus (AD 286–305) who abdicated with his colleague Diocletian.

Above right: A complete contrast in the Piazza Armerina mosaics is a group of bikini-clad young ladies who have been taking part

in some athletic contest and have been awarded their prizes of crowns and palm fronds.

Below right: An unusual representation in mosaic at the House of Dionysus, Paphos, Cyprus, is that of the old man Ikarius to whom Dionysus gave the secret of making wine. Sadly it caused his death at the hands of the enraged friends of two drunken peasants supposedly poisoned by the unaccustomed drink.

Lycurgus and Ambrosia, and so on. A charming composition shows young children hunting in the manner of their elders. One of the best known of this unusual series of mosaics is that in the Hall of the Ten Maidens. Here ten young girls shown in two registers and clad in what can only be described as 'bikinis' are carrying out gymnastic exercises. There is an element of competition since there are prizes. One girl has already received her victor's palm and wreath, which she is adjusting on her head, while another who holds what looks like a parasol, but which is actually the wheel of the game of circus races, is just being handed her wreath and palm.

Scattered throughout the empire there are a number of large villas where the provision of mosaics in large quantity, as at the Piazza Armerina, really raise questions as to who the original owner could have been, his wealth as well as interest that would lead him to commission so extensive a series. In Cyprus, within the area of Nea Paphos (New Paphos), a bulldozer levelling fields in the spring of 1962 uncovered mosaics belonging to a villa of the late Roman period. It had apparently been built early in the second century AD and lasted for just over 100 years until earthquakes in AD 332 and 342 destroyed it and much of the city. The site evidenced a

ΙΚΑΡΙΟΣ

Above left: The House of Dionysus at Paphos, Cyprus, a great Roman villa destroyed by earthquakes in the early fourth century AD, takes its name from the several representations of the god that occur there. Here he is seen reclining with the nymph Akme.

Above: One of the many fine mosaics of the second century from the great eastern city of Antioch-on-the-Orontes in Syria shows the perplexity of the young shepherd Paris when he

was called upon to judge between the three goddesses. Louvre, Paris.

Right: Trier, the capital of the northern late Empire, was a city with huge houses and resplendent mosaics. This third-century example shows the literary leanings of the owner in choosing to have the Nine Muses represented, although not all are definitely identified by their appropriate attributes. Rheinisches Landesmuseum, Trier.

long history, the first house probably being of the Hellenistic period, the second of the Flavian period in the last quarter of the first century AD, and then the last villa. Each later building seems to have mainly used the earlier walls for foundations and followed the same orientation. In this it shares features with other great houses of the Roman east in Ionia, Syria, especially at Antioch, and the Roman houses with their Hellenistic antecedents on Delos. This great villa discovered at Paphos has been called 'The House of Dionysus' because the god of wine is seen as the dominant figure in the second panel of mosaic concerned with mythological scenes, and he is also represented in several other places. The magnificence of the mosaics mark out the owner as a person of considerable wealth who obviously took a keen interest in the motifs that were being composed and laid on his splendid floors. He had an interest in Dionysus/Bacchus, the mythological traditions and also the wild-animal hunt.

The main panel with Dionysus presents the god and the mythological origin of wine. The central standing figure is identified as Icarius of Athens who had entertained Dionysus and been given the secret of how to cultivate the vine and make wine. Icarius took some skins of his first wine to offer to people to try. He is holding the reins of his two oxen who are pulling a two-wheeled cart loaded with the wine skins. Icarius holds out his right hand in a gesture toward the semidraped nymph Akme, seen toasting the young Dionysus who sits to the left wearing his vine wreath and holding a bunch of grapes. Behind the cart to the right are two young shepherds who have been offered wine and become drunk. One has already fallen down and is holding his head, the other is about to join him, buckling at the knees. Such was their state, according to the myth, that the shepherds' friends thought Icarius had poisoned them, so they killed him and threw his body down a well. Tragedy followed tragedy; his daughter Erigone, with his faithful dog Moera, found the body and hanged herself from a tree. Subsequently Icarius was changed into the star Bootes, Erigone into the constellation Virgo and the dog Moera became the Dog Star Canis.

On the east side of the great hall is featured the Triumph of Dionysus. This is a very popular subject in mosaics and even more so sculptured in deep relief, sometimes almost three-dimensional, on pagan sarcophagi since in the latter use it had overtones of a life to come for the deceased. Dionysus appears in his usual panther-drawn chariot and is attended by Pan, satyrs, devotees and a trumpeter to sound the god's triumph. Elsewhere in the villa many mythological subjects are treated, many of them having a link in being concerned with love, unrequited or otherwise. They include: Narcissus; Pyramus and Thisbe; Poseidon and Amyone; Apollo and Daphne; Hippolytus and Phaedra and also Ganymede and the Eagle (that is, Zeus who carried him off to act as his cupbearer). The same scene can be found far away in the villa at Bignor in Sussex. Obviously the owner liked and knew his myths but he also had harvesting scenes, the Seasons and the Great Hunt represented. All these are well-known topics, especially in North African mosaics and in Syria. A splendid and large mosaic from Antioch in Syria, one of many fine mosaics from the area, continues the mythological interest in representing the Judgment of Paris. The shepherd boy Paris who, by his choice between the

three goddesses and award of the golden apple to Venus, was to precipitate the Trojan War, is seen with the three delectable young women in a pleasant landscape. The story was, once again, widely popular and traces its artistic antecedents, of course, back to much earlier painting on Greek black- and red-figure pottery.

The arts, especially as represented by The Nine Muses, were favorite themes. A particularly fine series of the Nine Muses was found on a mosaic from a second-century villa at Trier in Germany. The city, capital of the northern reaches of Rome, is noted for its numerous fine and large mosaics. This one shows the Muses three by three and, while six can be immediately identified by the attributes with them, such as Thalia (Comedy) with her comic mask, Clio (History) with her scroll, and so on, the central one and last bottom two have no distinctive identification. It is a little curious to find the Nine so resplendently displayed so far north in the Roman empire where, at least for the owner, they appear to be as at home as in their original Greek setting.

Perhaps it is not remarkable, since human nature is so diverse, that in areas such as North Africa where some of the most gory representations of bloody combats are found, mosaics of a much more humanitarian nature also occur. Mythological subjects have been noted as being widely favored and shown with varying degrees of skill, but literature itself, often based on these same topics, is also to be found. The *Aeneid*, the great epic poem by Virgil, had many events in it that lent themselves for illustration in the villa of a literary-minded owner. In the Maison de l'Arsenal (also known as the Maison du Virgile), in Tunisia at Sousse, a panel in one floor showed the owner's undoubted devotion to the greatest Latin poet. A very carefully executed portrait shows a seated man looking half to his right and holding a partly opened scroll on his knee. The portrait, for such it seems from the detail, is not identified, presumably because it was immediately recognizable. The lines on the scroll merely serve to confirm the identification, they read: 'Musa mihi causas memora quo numine laeso Quidve . . .', the opening words of *Aeneid* I, 8. The divine inspiration they underline is seen in the two Muses that stand one on either side of Virgil; on the right Melpomene (Tragedy), with a tragic mask, and on the left Clio (History), with her unfurled scroll.

The Virgilian connection with North Africa is obvious enough, as much of the story is centered there when Aeneas arrives from the sack of Troy and meets Dido, Queen of Carthage. It is, however, curious to find a number of the episodes from *Aeneid* books I and IV represented on a large scale on the mosaic from the cold bath (*frigidarium*) at the villa at Low Ham in north Somerset. Once again, it is obvious that the owner was familiar with Virgil but how did such a design and sequence of illustrations come to be brought to his notice? The technique and execution of the mosaic is

certainly by a provincial hand but the pictures must have come from a pattern book imported from North Africa or, rather more unlikely, from an illustrated copy of Virgil. The closest parallel here is the Codex Vaticanus Latinus in the Vatican with its series of painted miniatures scattered throughout the text. In this mosaic we see the goddess Venus in the center flanked by a pair of cupids – once more it is the love theme, unrequited, that appears so many times in mosaics. Around the goddess the other four panels show, on the right, the arrival of the Trojan fleet off Carthage; above, Venus stirring love in the hearts of Aeneas and Dido; on the left, the pair go hunting and, below, the lovers embrace between a pair of wind-blown trees (actually in a cave in *Aeneid* IV where they shelter from a storm). The whole design of the mosaic was laid out for it to be viewed from outside its area, from an ambulatory which would have been normal in a North African villa but which here does not exist as the mosaic pressed close to the bath house walls.

Above left: Literary allusions occur in mosaics throughout the Empire but only in this early third century mosaic from Sousse do we find the poet Virgil although elements from his works are often shown. Bardo Museum, Tunis.

Left: The large mosaic from the baths at Low Ham, Somerset, is obviously from the repertoire and pattern book of a North African mosaicist. How it came to be chosen and laid so far from its origins is a mystery. Taunton Castle Museum, Somerset.

Right: Zeus' escapades with various ladies were a favorite subject in many spheres of art. A mosaic in the villa at Lullingstone, Kent, shows him in one of his many disguises as a bull carrying off a rather unconcerned Europa.

Below: At the Chedworth villa, Gloucestershire, Winter is shown as an appealing little fellow well wrapped up against the local conditions in his hood, tunic and boots.

Another allusion to Virgil in Roman Britain at about the same date as Low Ham, in the mid-fourth century AD, is on a mosaic at Lullingstone, Kent. Here is a scene of Europa being carried away over the waves on the back of the bull (Jupiter in disguise) while one cupid figure waves the bull onward another hangs onto its tail. The couplet above it – 'invida si ta[uri] vidisset Iuno natatus/iustius Aeolias isset adusque domos' (had jealous Juno seen the swimming bull she would have rightly gone to the halls of Aeolus the god of the winds) – is a direct allusion to *Aeneid* I where she tried to persuade Aeolus to overwhelm Aeneas in a storm before he could reach Italy. Interestingly, the couplet is in Ovidian meter.

Literary and mythological allusions could travel the empire to find representation in mosaics and be essentially little changed. Where local differences do show up strongly is in the popular representations of the seasons. Spring in most areas would be seen in much the same way as would harvest, with the ripe corn in her hair, but the representation of winter varies with the climate. A calendar mosaic from El Djem illustrates each month in a lively little vignette, but other mosaics that show the four seasons alone (generally in the corners) usually have four female busts only identifiable by their attributes. In the cold northern empire, winter is well-protected, like the amusing little fellow at Chedworth, Gloucestershire, with his hood, cloak, heavy tunic, leggings and carrying a dead hare and a bare branch. The female personification of the same season at Bignor is likewise heavily muffled up.

Left: It is thought that the youthful central figure with the Christian chi-rho symbol behind his head in the center of the mosaic excavated at Hinton St Mary, Dorset, represents Christ. The figures in the four corners would then be the four Evangelists and the representations between them in the lunettes are allusions to the Tree of Life and the paradise of the next world. British Museum, London.

Right: An Evangelist carrying a processional cross and an open Gospel book is realistically depicted in a lunette in the mausoleum of Galla Placidia at Ravenna.

Above: Baptism by immersion led, in North Africa, to elaborate baptismal tanks being provided with steps leading down into them and the sides being ornately decorated in mosaic, often with a dedication, as here at Sbeitla, Tunisia.

Right: In the mausoleum of Galla Placidia at Ravenna a cupboard shown open with the four Gospels laid, labelled, on the shelves represents graphically 'The new treasure of the Gospels.'

A new feature in mosaics in the fourth century, after Constantine's Edict of Toleration in AD 313, is the emergence of Christian motifs. This is particularly evident in places such as Ravenna in northern Italy, in the heavily Christian cities of North Africa and in the eastern provinces. Many more of these mosaics are found on the walls and in the apses of churches and are generally best known from the later glories of the huge Byzantine vaults with their glowing colors. One of the most interesting and earliest of these mosaics is a portion which survived in the mausoleum of the Julii, excavated beneath St Peter's, Rome. It dates from the mid-third century and represents Christ-Helios in a chariot drawn by white horses, a well-known assimilation in early Christian art and iconography, and not

untoward as a similar conflation of Christ-Orpheus is also well known. Christ himself is seen portrayed with the chi-rho symbol (the early Christian 'secret sign' made up of the first two letters in Greek of his name) behind his head at the center of the mosaic from Hinton St Mary. He is flanked by two pomegranates, a symbol of life. The apparently pagan hunting scenes in the lunettes around the mosaic can be interpreted as the teeming life of Paradise and the great roundel of Bellerophon vanquishing the chimaera on winged Pegasus as good overcoming evil. The strange thing about this mosaic is that with such a representation of Christ in the center it could be expected to be more appropriate to a wall or vault mosaic rather than the floor where it would be trodden on.

Left: The vaults of the ambulatory in the mausoleum/church of Constantina, 'Santa Costanza,' Rome, are covered in mosaics of the second quarter of the fourth century AD.

Above: Vintaging scenes, originally a favorite pagan motif, are easily taken over into the Christian repertoire, as in this detail of the grape harvest being carried off from the vault in the mausoleum/church of Santa Costanza, Rome.

Many Christian dedications in mosaic occur in the North African cities so influenced by the writings of St Augustine and Tertullian. Their texts and symbols immediately identify them; splendidly decorated mosaic baptisteries were common and many of them are still *in situ.* They were generally four-lobed in their layout, and deep for baptism by total immersion. Some have steps covered in mosaic for the initiate to enter and leave by, as at Sbeitla. The scene of the baptism of Christ by St John the Baptist is featured at the center of the dome of the mid-fifth-century AD Baptistery of the Orthodox at Ravenna, surrounded by a procession of saints. Of particular note is the skillful way that the artist has created the illusion of Christ standing in the clear waters of the Jordan. The building itself, let alone its superb interior mosaics, is generally acknowledged to be probably the best preserved of all early Christian buildings.

Another building with a gem-like interior at Ravenna

that is some 25 years earlier is the Mausoleum of Galla Placidia. The predominantly blue mosaics are softly lit through thin alabaster windows. They are a deep blue against which the stars and white figures of the saints seem to hover suspended. One mosaic shows a cupboard in which are seen four codices identified as being of the Evangelists, and hence the complete work represents 'the new treasure of the Gospels.'

The church of S Costanza in Rome, built by the emperor Constantine for members of his family, brings the wheel full circle in a way because there we can see the strong links between Christian mosaic art and the earlier traditions, motifs and iconography. The vault is rich in scenes of vintaging that are pagan and Dionysiac – cupids picking grapes, carts laden with grapes and men treading grapes. The scatter of birds, twigs, drinking vessels and so on, on one part of the vault readily brings to mind the 'unswept floor' (*asaraton*) ascribed to Sosos of Pergamon. The same vintaging reliefs appear on the great red stone porphyry sarcophagus that once stood here. Old motifs that can be traced back centuries as far as fourth-century BC Greece have become transformed under the acceptance of the new religion and then go forward to become part of some of the finest mosaic treasures that have survived from the later Byzantine world, the eastern Roman empire.

4. Wallpaintings and Frescoes

Rare painted wooden tondo of *c* AD 190 showing Septimius Severus and his family – Julia Domna, Caracalla and Geta. (Note that the face of Geta has been hacked out; this was done after his murder by his brother Caracalla in 212 and his images were ordered to be removed.) Found in Egypt. Such representations of the Imperial family must have been common in wallpaintings. Staatliche Museen, Preussischer Kulturbesitz, Berlin.

By reason of their age and fragile nature, it will be no surprise that the major examples of Roman wall paintings that do survive, especially figured examples, come from the Campania, from the buried cities of Pompeii and Herculaneum. These are followed by examples from Rome itself. By comparison, elsewhere in the empire little survives; odd pieces of 'inhabited' scrollwork, birds, foliage, and so on, or just sweeps of plain colors with perhaps a dado finish. Similarly, and for much the same reasons, actual paintings on wood are virtually nonexistent – they need the special circumstances of environment, such as the dry sands of Egypt, for them to be preserved. This is not to say that ordinary paintings, as against wood paintings, were not carried out in antiquity; they were, and we have numerous descriptions of many that crammed the temples from writings by such as Pausanias, the indefatigable traveller who wrote his 'Guide to Greece' in the mid-second century AD, detailing the statues, paintings and other wonders that he saw. From such descriptions it is possible at times to recognize the precursor or ancestor of an extant wall painting or mosaic which has been later copied in this different medium – a case in point is the famous mosaic of the battle of Issus between Alexander the Great and Darius that was found in the House of the Faun at Pompeii.

This is copied from the painting by Philoxenos, long since lost. Considering the hazards of the centuries it is surprising that so much of this form of Roman art has survived, but it is only largely because of its having been overwhelmed by the natural disaster of a volcanic eruption.

Wall paintings were used for decoration long before the world of Greece and Rome. The brightly colored paintings of daily life on the walls of ancient Egyptian tombs are well enough known; these date mainly to the second half of the second millennium BC but the earliest example, 'The Painted Tomb' found at Hierakonpolis, dates from *circa* 3400 BC. From Europe the frescoes of the Cretan palaces of the Middle and Early Late Minoan period (*circa* 1900–1500 BC) are bright with color, people, plants and fishes. The essential difference between the Egyptian and the Cretan painting, wall paintings and frescoes, is one of technique: wall painting is done on a dry surface, fresco is executed rapidly on wet plaster (as Michelangelo's Sistine Chapel). By virtue of the need for speed, coupled with an accuracy of line, fresco painting tends to be more alive.

The Romans mostly used wall painting, as against fresco (although a report by the Instituto Centrale dell

Left: Lifesize wooden mummy board painted in wax encaustic on linen showing the dead youth's mummy and himself dressed as in life being greeted by Anubis, the jackal-headed god of embalming. It is from such paintings (some are known on linen) and the panel portraits from Egypt that the best idea of what may have existed in private houses of this nature elsewhere in the Empire is obtained. Louvre, Paris.

Right: An unusual wallpainting from Rome showing builders at work and the use of scaffolding which would be needed in the plastering of walls to prepare them to receive their painted decoration.

Below: Wallpainting on the exterior wall of the clothworker M. Vecilio Verecondo in the Via dell' Abbondanzia, Pompeii, showing the various processes involved in the cloth production.

Restauro, Rome, concerned with Pompeian painting has suggested that there is some evidence for the use of fresco, certainly the fluidity of line suggests that technique in many instances). They built on the experience and methods of the earlier craftsmen but they had the benefit of better knowledge of the basic materials involved and their chemical behavior. The essential reason why the colors have remained so bright over the centuries is because of the ingredients used. The pigments were obtained from natural sources, minerals essentially, some vegetable and animal. Both Pliny and Vitruvius have a lot to say about the pigments, the best sources and the best methods of applying them. The mineral-based pigments survive the best and they are obtained by grinding down ochres and so on, and

applying them in suspension, possibly using something such as albumen (white of egg) as a medium. White was obtained from crushed and calcinated marble or oyster shells and black was natural carbon, for example lamp black or from burned wood, mixed with size.

The preparation of the plaster surface of the wall to be painted was of the utmost importance. Again, detailed instructions are given in Vitruvius. The wall was normally plastered in sections from the top to the bottom. Several coats of plaster would be applied, each succeeding one after the underlying coat had partly dried. This served to give it a bonding. On large stretches of wall scaffolding was used and the plaster applied in horizontal bands, which was rather difficult because if the upper band dried quickly horizontal ridges would be apparent where the next section started. A most unusual wallpainting from a house in Rome actually shows scaffolding in use, but here the men are building the house as against using it for plastering the wall – a very strange subject on the part of the house owner to choose to decorate his walls unless, of course, he was a successful master builder himself.

Once the several layers of plaster were laid the final, upper layer was often burnished or polished, using a stone burnisher. The addition of fine kaolin to the mixture for the final layer would help it respond to such polishing. As Vitruvius remarks in his Book VII, 'they will show a glittering splendor when the colors are laid on with the last coat.' The background color laid in this fashion was often put on the wet plaster, fresco technique, and responded well to the burnishing treatment, as examples from the Campanian cities show.

Before looking at some of the examples of wall painting surviving from wealthy house interiors, it should be

Right : A fine example of Pompeian wallpainting from the cubiculum of the villa of Fannius Sinistor at Boscoreale. The perspective achieved in both the landscape and the architectural panels is to be particularly noted. The Metropolitan Museum of Art, New York, Rogers Fund 1903.

Above : Wallpainting now preserved underground in the Golden House of Nero close to the Colosseum, Rome. They present a 'picture within a picture' with the framed views within their painted architectural setting.

remembered that there are different levels (classes in a way) of wall painting that have survived. This is especially evident at Pompeii, notably in the long commercial road known as the Via dell 'Abbondanza. It was a street that bisected Pompeii, running west to east from the Forum to the Porta Sarno, and was an important thoroughfare, one of the two *decumani* (the other is the Via di Nola). There were a number of shops along the street, principally small 'fast food' types or bars. At the Forum end of the street M Vecilio Verecundus, a maker of cloth, woollen clothing and felt articles had his premises. The entrance is decorated with a 'shop sign,' a wall painting, showing the feltmakers hard at work and, to the right, the final product being held up for the customer's inspection. Another painting close by shows the workroom's patron deities, Venus Pompeiana being drawn along in a quadriga of elephants; she is also the embodiment of Aphrodite-Isis (the latter a goddess with a fine temple in Pompeii) and is accompanied on either side by female personifications of the city carrying cornucopiae (horns of plenty). Beside the painting is another of Mercury carrying his caduceas and wearing his winged hat and sandals. Here he is not so much the messenger of the gods as the patron god of commerce. Graffiti on the walls refer to the forthcoming gladiatorial combat shows in the amphitheater and the fact that the upper tiers will have awnings provided as protection against the hot sun. Such paintings are on a totally different level from what is generally thought of as Roman wall painting, the luxurious provision by wealthy citizens.

As will have become evident, most of the finest Roman wall painting extant not only comes from Italy but dates essentially from before AD 79. There are basically two types, the first concerned largely with shapes, geometrical and architectural, the second with

representing people (be they from legend, religion or everyday life) and objects. The Styles of painting at Pompeii were first outlined by August Mau in 1882. He identified four successive Styles. His first Masonry Style appears at Pompeii in the early first century BC; as its name indicates, it emphasized jointed stone masonry in bright colors. The second Architectural Style follows on from about 80 BC, developing the idea of depth and perspective on the wall, endeavoring to lose the solidity of the wall by effects. Frameworks are used around subjects and about 50–25 BC the architectural frameworks take over, whole walls are developed and painted with architectural views, cleverly three-dimensional in their effect. One of the best examples of this comes from the villa of Fannius Sinistor at Boscoreale (now in the Metropolitan Museum, New York). In the foreground to the right a delicately garlanded pillar stands tall beside an ornamental double door to a house (note the splendid detail of the animal-head doorknockers). Rising away behind it are terraces with houses, tiled roofs at different angles, and a long colonnaded building right in the background. The whole is brilliantly conceived and can be dated around 40 BC. Other representations of the Architectural Style delight in *scaena frons* (stage props), that may still be seen for real at some of the great theaters in North Africa, such as at rebuilt Sabratha. Within these decorative and complex structural representations are frames, like pictures hung on a wall, often with mythological or legendary subjects represented.

With the Third Style there is a return to simpler, more rigid symmetry, the three-dimensional perspective illusion is renounced. It uses strong bands of color for effect. This Style continues in use, overlapping to a certain extent with the Second Style, until *circa* AD 50. Thereafter follows the Fourth Style, the last at Pompeii before the earthquake of AD 62. Here the walls are almost 'color washed' and delicate tracery patterns painted on the background. Naturally there are overlaps between the four styles, and it is not unusual to find more than one Style in a house, given that it was occupied over a period of time.

Much of the subject matter and style of representation of the subjects seen in Roman wall painting sees its origins in Hellenistic painting and, in some instances, can be traced back to lost Greek works of the fourth and third centuries BC. It is, in many instances, only the skill of the individual artist concerned that either gives us a reasonable copy with understanding of the original, still with its Greek overtones, or presents a pedestrian reproduction that has lost all the verve and spontaneity of the original, leaving unbalanced, wooden figures within a surround. As may be expected, the artists working at a wealthy citizen's or at imperial command in Rome were superior to those employed at Pompeii and Herculaneum. Curiously, it was the rediscovery of the Golden House of Nero (the Domus

Above: Wallpainting from a villa at Stabiae on the Bay of Naples showing a seaside view of Puteoli, another of the small towns destroyed in the catastrophic eruption of AD 79. Museo Nazionale, Naples.

Right: The fresco of a wild garden with birds and fruit trees from the empress Livia's villa at Prima Porta is a masterpiece of both observation and rapid painting in view of the technique used. Museo Nazionale, Rome.

Aurea) in the Renaissance that caught the imagination of a number of artists such as Raphael who penetrated the underground grottoes in the hillside close by the Colosseum. They were captivated by the fine tendril forms and copied them for use as decoration. Because of their origins in the 'grottoes' they came to be called 'grotesques.' Nero's Golden House survived because the area was turned into a public pleasure garden after his suicide and official damnation by the Senate. Subsequently the Colosseum was built over parts of the area. There are two distinct spheres of decoration: one is the fine linear tracery and floral decoration that runs along the ceilings of the corridors and high vaults with scattered charming little vignettes (framed in ornamental outlines) of things such as lively seahorses and mermen. They are rendered in an almost impressionistic style. The second sphere of decoration employs more of the Hellenistic tradition of wooden panel paintings, rich in color and using highlights and shadows (chiaroscuro) to achieve remarkable effects. Its use in Roman painting occurs in Nero's Golden House for the first time and, with the fluidity of the other little vignettes, has had a continuing influence even into modern times.

A particular feature was the use of *trompe-l'oeil*, particularly in niches, to give the impression of a window. Its use in a private house is well seen in the house found near the Farnesina, Rome. Here a wall was decorated with *trompe-l'oeil* architecture in a most effective manner. Into, or onto, this has been set a number of painted imitation pictures in various frames. According to the 'Styles' criteria the wall itself is in advanced Second Style while the paintings added on are in the so-called Severe Style of the mid-fifth century BC at a point of transition between Archaic and Classical art. The figures are drawn with an economy of line, with slight touches of color, on a white background. Their closest parallels lie in the drawing on Athenian White-ground lekythoi (tall handled jugs) which generally had a funerary purpose.

From the southern cities similar 'framed' pictures are known. One of the most interesting among a series of landscapes and architectural details is a painting of a villa beside the sea from Stabiae, one of the towns on the Bay of Naples overcome at the same time as Pompeii and Herculaneum. The roundel shows the façade of a *villa marittima*, its colonnaded façade curv-ing inward, above which is a central tower. Two jetties project into the sea before the villa and it must have been from such a villa as this that the Elder Pliny set forth to investigate the catastrophe and was overcome. The roundel, and a companion piece, came from a Fourth Style setting akin to the Farnesina *trompe-l'oeil*. In contrast to the careful architectural delineation is the painting of a garden scene that decorated one wall in the main salon of Livia's villa at Prima Porta, just outside Rome (the empress Livia was the wife of Augustus). Although from her villa, it is possible that it was painted after her death in AD 29. The style, quality and content of this painting, actually a fresco, make it unique. The use of fresco technique has produced marvellous effects; shading of blues in the sky against which birds are seen perching on branches and pecking at berries or fruit. An interesting feature of the garden is the fact that it is shown fenced round by a trelliswork. This is very un-Roman and has its precedents in Western Asia. This painting produces the best parallel as an illustration for what the carefully laid out garden found at the palace at Fishbourne, Hampshire, England, might have looked like.

Among the most interesting of the surviving paintings are those that show aspects of life rather than the heavy emphasis on myth and legend. One of the most potent of the former genre is a painting found in a house near the theater at Pompeii. It depicts the riot that took place in the amphitheater in AD 59. This erupted after a gladiatorial show, and a number of visitors from Nuceria were either killed or wounded. It caused a great scandal and reached the ears of the Senate in Rome. As a consequence Nero closed the amphitheater for ten years – a harsh sentence akin to closing a major football stadium nowadays. (The amphitheater was badly damaged in the earthquake of AD 62 and, along with the temple of Isis, was the only public building fully restored by the eruption of AD 79.) In the painting small figures dart across and around the amphitheater and a graffito is known from another house with a triumphant gladiator waving a palm branch and referring to the riot.

On a more peaceful and homely note is the famous

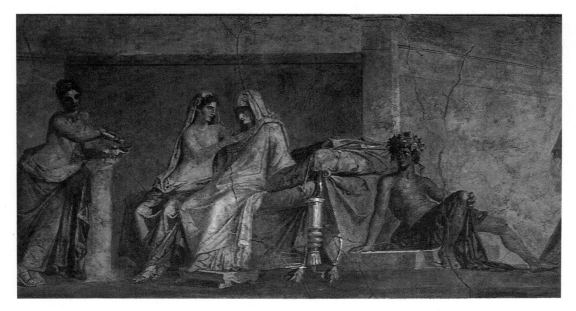

Above: A most unusual wall-painting from Pompeii illustrates an actual event, the riot in the amphitheater at Pompeii in AD 59 after which Nero closed the establishment for ten years. Of particular interest is the attempt at perspective to show the rioting taking place both inside and outside the amphitheater. Museo Nazionale, Naples.

Left: 'The Music Lesson,' from Pompeii, is a charming study of a young girl being taught to play the lyre. British Museum, London.

Below left: The so-called Aldobrandini Wedding early first century AD wallpainting has been noted as a fine work of art since it was first discovered in 1604. Museo Profano, Vatican.

Above right: Often referred to as 'The Baker and his Wife,' this Fourth Style painting of a young couple from Pompeii more probably represents a minor magistrate, Proculus, and his young wife. Museo Nazionale, Naples.

Below right: Wall painting portrait of a young girl holding a writing tablet and a stylus (for writing, scratching, in the wax on the tablet boards). A delightful study that is often called 'Sappho,' after the Greek poetess. From Pompeii. Museo Nazionale, Naples.

Aldobrandini Wedding, a wall painting of the Augustan period found on the Esquiline Hill in Rome as long ago as 1604 and acknowledged as a masterpiece ever since. It shows the preparations for an upper-class Roman marriage but also incorporates religious and mystical symbolism among the figures portrayed around the bride-to-be. The bride sits in contemplative mood in the center of the picture, apparently being calmed or comforted by the half-draped female beside her. Behind the couch a youth with a Dionysiac wreath on his head casts an anxious glance toward the pair. A similar, quietly pleasing scene is the 'Music Lesson' from Pompeii where a garlanded young man is teaching a young girl to play the lyre as they sit side by side on a light double couch. A draped figure – goddess or chaperone ? – leans nonchalantly on a pillar watching them.

A charming study of a couple, a young man and his wife, is often referred to as 'The Baker and his Wife' because the house where it was found (on the back wall of a small hall off the atrium) belonged to someone involved in baking. The identification of the young man as a minor magistrate, because of the toga he wears and the red-sealed scroll he rests against his chin, seems rather more appropriate. The young woman holds a double-leaf writing tablet and presses a stylus against her lips. Although at first glance it might seem that some indication of literary leanings was implied this may not be so as the pose is rather a conventional one known from elsewhere. The couple both have a distant, faraway look, and their eyes gaze out and past the viewer. Their similarity to a number of the surviving wax encaustic portraits on wooden boards from Egypt (principally the area of the Fayuum) is very striking, although this couple are of slightly earlier date.

The emphasis on aspects of daily life can also be seen in a number of wall paintings from tombs; the children at play with ball and trundle cart from a tomb on the Via Portuense, Rome, can be contrasted with the display of solid wealth represented in the detailed depiction of a silver dinner service on a table from the tomb of Vestorius Priscus at Pompeii. This painting is of particular interest in the parallels it shows with some of the actual pieces of contemporary silverware found at Boscoreale.

Other aspects of daily life, but in a humorous vein, are the series of amorini (little cupids) shown in a frieze from the House of the Vettii at Pompeii. We see them carrying out all sorts of tasks including working as pharmacists, wine merchants, jewellers and metal smiths and even apparently striking coins as moneyers. These amusing little fellows are actually quite small in relation to the many other fine paintings that exist in this house belonging to the two wealthy merchants Aulus Vettius Restitutus and Conviva. The house is one of the best in Pompeii with its many illustrations taken from myth and legend: Leda and the swan; Poseidon and Amymone; Hercules and the serpents; Daedalus showing Pasiphae the wooden cow, and so on. Scenes from the great epic poems, Ulysses and his various adventures in the *Odyssey*, Aeneas and his encounters in the *Aeneid*, were all very popular motifs as wall paintings.

Below: The House of the Vettii at Pompeii has one of the most remarkable series of wallpaintings found in the town. They are of high quality and cover a vast range of subjects from mythology to daily life and include amusing little scenes such as this where cupids work as moneyers striking coins. It is part of a long and narrow frieze showing cupids engaged in various pursuits and is merely an adjunct to the larger area of the painted wall above it.

Right: A wallpainting representing a scene from Virgil's *Aeneid* from Pompeii showing the doctor Iapis using forceps to tend an arrow wound in Aeneas' leg. Aeneas has his arm round the shoulders of his young son Ascanias while his protecting goddess Aphrodite (Venus) looks on. Museo Nazionale, Naples.

In a different category are those paintings that are concerned with the religion of the day. Some of the best surviving examples relate to the cult of the Egyptian goddess Isis. In Rome there is the Hall of Isis (*Aula Isiaca*) on the Palatine Hill which was decorated with scenes from the Isis legend and emblems of her cult. This was preserved by being built over during Nero's reign and subsequently buried in the foundations of the basilica of the great Flavian palace. At about the same time, other Isiac paintings were being buried in different circumstances as the recently rebuilt temple of the goddess was overcome at Pompeii. A series of wall paintings from there show different aspects and rituals of the cult. A particularly well known piece shows the shaven-headed priests performing the daily ritual before a chorus of worshippers. A priest tends the lit altar while herons (supposedly the sacred ibis) strut about it and a high priest stands at the top of the steps flanked by junior priests holding the goddess' sacred instrument, the sistrum, a pleasantly tinkling metallic rattle.

Above: An episode from the *Odyssey* where Odysseus hears the Sirens' song but does not succumb to their lure because he has been tied to his ship's mast and his sailors' ears stuffed with wax. This was a very popular subject in wall paintings and other media. From Pompeii. British Museum, London.

Left: The enigmatic series of wallpaintings gives the name to the Villa of the Mysteries just outside the walls of Pompeii. This detail, showing a winged goddess about to lash the bare back of a woman who buries her head in the lap of her companion, is a very effective composition in continuing the sequence of events across the corner of the room.

Above: The Eastern or Oriental cults were well represented in Pompeii. This wallpainting shows the early morning ceremonies in honor of the Egyptian goddess Isis, whose temple there is the best preserved example of the cult in the Roman world. Of the Roman poets, several especially satirized the shaven-headed priests of the goddess clearly seen here. Museo Nazionale, Naples.

Many religions were represented at Pompeii and Herculaneum in wall painting and one of the best known examples, still *in situ*, occurs in the Villa of the Mysteries just outside the Herculaneum Gate. This large villa had a chequered history from the third century BC, starting as a town house, developing into a manor and then declining into a farmhouse. Its principal interest lies in the large room painted in the first century BC in the Second Style with a series of scenes that pass right round the room. Twenty-four almost

Above: The unusual wallpaintings in the little Christian chapel that had been made from a room in the villa at Lullingstone, Kent, were dominated by the symbolism of the chi-rho monogram, flanked by A (alpha) and W (omega) – the beginning and the end. British Museum, London.

Right: A series of figures of worshippers at the Lullingstone villa, Kent, were shown in the wallpaintings standing with arms open in the typical *orans* position of a person praying. British Museum, London.

Below: Wallpaintings with Christian significance are to be expected and are more commonly found in the catacombs in the third and fourth centuries. A typical example from the catacomb of the Aurelii, Rome, shows the Twelve Apostles in a funerary niche and a pair of peacocks, symbolic of eternal life, below. Other such scenes show the Last Supper and several of Christ's miracles.

lifesize figures associated with Dionysiac worship (hence the villa's name) form eight scenes which have been interpreted as recording the initiation of a rather frightened young woman into the mysteries of the cult. However, such mysteries were secret and their representation in a large, well-lit room with a picture window looking out across the villa's portico to the Bay of Naples is not very supportive of the idea. More likely is the interpretation of the series of scenes as the prepara-

tion of a bride for marriage and the symbolic rituals that would be entailed.

Definitely religious in tone, however, are the rare wall paintings found at the Lullingstone Villa, Kent, associated with a third-century Christian chapel showing a series of *orans* in the attitude of prayer with hands outstretched and a large chi-rho symbol framed between painted pillars. These paintings on the frontiers of empire are a far reflection of the whole series of

paintings with scenes from the Bible and the Apostles which occur in the catacombs along the Appian Way.

Roman wall painting has, by this late date, changed its whole approach and iconography. Once more, as with the mosaics, the official acceptance of Christianity brings about changes that leave the old favorite subjects behind and which look forward to a flowering of Christian wall paintings in the Byzantine and later periods.

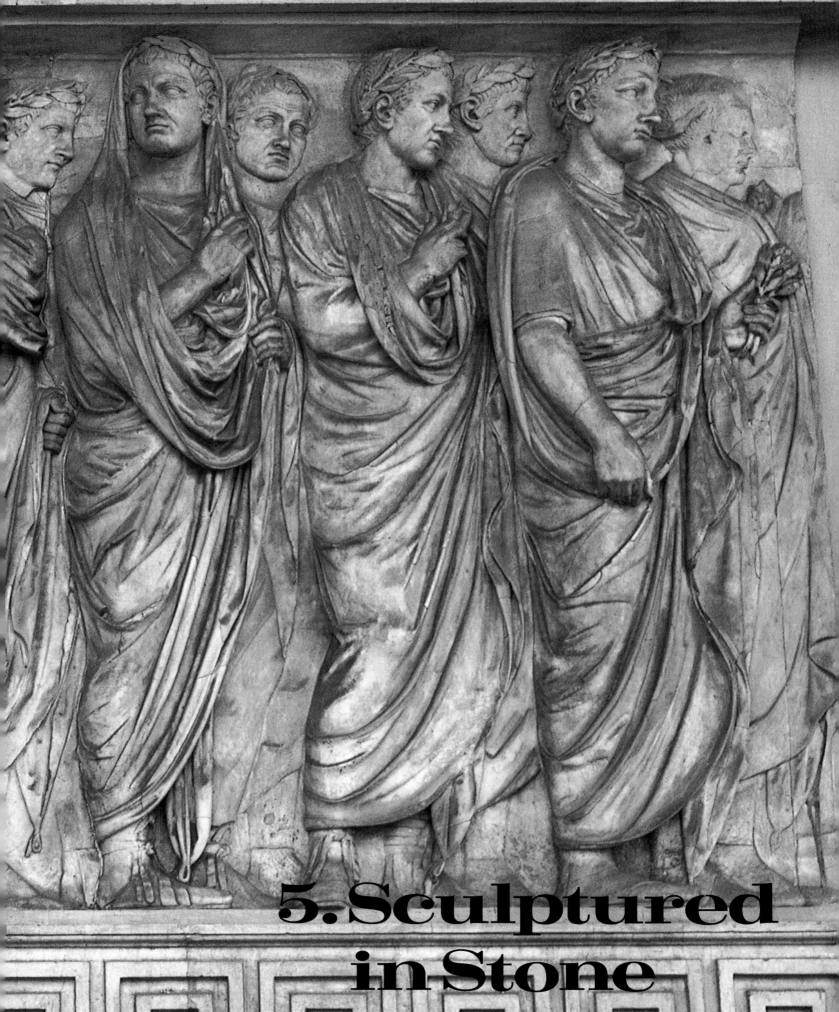

5. Sculptured in Stone

After architecture the epitome of Roman civilization is its sculpture. Many nations of antiquity attained great heights in their sculpture and their mastery of hard stones, achieving superb finishes and details that a modern sculptor would be hard pressed to match. This is particularly true of ancient Egypt, where the hardest stones were worked with apparent ease as early as the beginning of the fourth millennium BC. The Mediterranean world was more concerned with the softer and easier to work marbles. As the might of Rome spread and it absorbed so many of these areas with long stoneworking traditions (and the quarries of different types of stone to go with them), great variations in approach to similar subjects or representations are found from one end of the empire to the other. While the basic motif employed might be typically Roman, its rendition, say, at the hands of a sculptor in Rome and one brought up in the eastern tradition of the Levant would almost certainly find the former having harsher, stronger lines and the latter a more flowing, softer line approach.

The quest for suitable stone to embellish temples, public buildings and houses, be it for freestanding statues or reliefs, was pursued throughout the empire. Rare and unusual stone would perhaps be shipped at great expense thousands of miles from the quarry where it might be known to occur. The quarries of the Red Sea Mountains were a favorite source of more exotic hardstones, and the distinctive red porphyry from the quarries at Aswan in southern Egypt was especially prized. The majority of surviving Roman stone sculpture is in marble, and the amount that does survive, be it three-dimensional busts and figures or two-dimensional reliefs, is nothing short of fantastic. This huge legacy can only represent a tiny fraction of what was once produced. So much has been destroyed over the centuries, either by acts of wanton destruction or the simple need to convert a ready supply of convenient pieces of marble into lime by burning it in a kiln, that we must be grateful for the large amount still surviving. Obviously out of the many thousands of pieces scattered throughout the public and private collections of the world some stand out as premier objects, masterpieces in their own right; others, perhaps not of the same class or quality can, nevertheless, take their turn alongside because of what they can tell us. This is essentially true of relief sculpture, be it panels to decorate some religious structure such as an altar or the representations of myth and legend and daily life to be found on the sides of sarcophagi decorated to please a wealthy owner.

Marble, as had been said, was largely used for Roman stone sculpture. This was quarried extensively from quarries that at first seem to have been privately owned. They were not, in the main, new quarries but had been extensively worked under the Greeks and during the Hellenistic period. Under the empire their ownership passed into the State's hands – so much official sculpture was required that it was obviously better to own and control the source. There were three main types of white marble in use for Roman sculpture: Pentalic, Parian and Luna. Pentalic marble came from near Athens, a fine-grained stone that was easy to work and which produced a pleasing goldish patina over the years. It had been highly esteemed in Greece. Parian marble was quarried on the island of Paros, part of the Cyclades group in the south Aegean Sea, and differed in having a large crystalline structure and was brilliant white. Luna marble, called after its location at Luni in the Apuan Alps of north Italy, has since become better known as Carrara marble, and was much favored by Michelangelo. Like Pentalic, Luna marble is fine grained, and it was from this stone that Trajan's Column was carved. These three were the main marbles but many others were used, being especially chosen for the variant colors and hues that occurred in different regions.

The extraction of marble from the quarries has not changed very much since Roman times. The technique was the same for most stones, from the hard granites in the quarries of Aswan to those of the softer Mediterranean marbles. An initial, narrow trench, laboriously cut, separated off a piece of stone of the required dimensions. Narrow wedges, cut in line, were used; they probably had blocks of wood forced into them which, when moistened, expanded and split the rock away. The piece of stone could be roughed out first in the quarry before being shipped by sea to its destination where the final carving would be done and finish be applied. In recent years, several shipwrecks with such unfinished stone cargoes have been excavated underwater and have indicated the extent of the trade. One ship was carrying a cargo of huge unfinished stone sarcophagi from Asia Minor to Rome when it foundered.

The finishing at the destination brought into play tools and instruments that are still used in the stone mason's craft: the hammer and chisel; a five-toothed claw chisel; positers; punches; gravers and so on. Final finish or high polish would be obtained by first rasping the surface and then using fine abrasives to achieve the required degree of polish. As is seen especially on sarcophagi reliefs with animated scenes and in the often highly ornamental hairstyles of ladies, a bow drill was used to facilitate deep cutting and an almost three-dimensional effect in some instances.

Much early Roman sculpture, as may be expected, looked back to its predecessor in Italy, the Etruscan civilization which Rome had been at such pains to stamp out. This is particularly evident in bronzework and terracottas as well as in stone sculpture. As the Roman empire expanded into the Hellenistic East there was a demand for statues and busts that followed the styles of that area. This demand was now becoming different; whereas earlier most sculpture was required

for religious use, or in a religious context such as tomb stele, now its acquisition was a proper mark of one's breeding and learning – it was needed for private use for the embellishment of the home. This in turn created a demand for copies of well-known and liked earlier masterpieces, either from the Archaic and Classical Greek schools or more recent Hellenistic compositions. Many of these Roman copies survive and, although properly speaking they are not Roman sculpture, they serve a very useful purpose in that they can be identified as copies of the work of known artists and sculptors from the literary descriptions that have come down to us. Numerous of these are copies of bronze originals, not stone originals. This created problems for the copyist sculptor because the stone could not sustain unsuspended weight in the same way that a cast metal statue could and therefore at times rather unsightly supports or armitures had to be incorporated into the stone copy for it to be able to stand.

The *marmorari* (marble sculptors) are known to have travelled widely to carry out commissions and in some instances we have evidence from inscriptions that record the details of where the particular sculptor came from. In the majority of cases, however, it is the style and technique used for particular pieces which reveals to the trained eye that the sculptor came from a different part of the empire.

As previously mentioned, early Roman stone sculpture in Italy itself owed quite a lot to the Etruscans. It fell into two groups: sculpture in the round – statues, busts and the like – and relief sculpture. At first reliefs were principally used to embellish religious and official buildings, and subsequently extensively used for funerary monuments and sarcophagi. The cult of the ancestor gave rise to some of the earliest sculptural Roman busts. It was the custom to keep busts or plaster death masks of ancestors, especially illustrious ones, in the house. These would be carried in the flamboyant funerary processions so that all would see the noble lineage of the deceased who had just joined his ancestors. Plaster busts and masks were used at first but, with wealth and the right craftsmen to be commissioned, stone took over. A striking example illustrating this is the stone statue in the Palazzo dei Conservatori (often incorrectly labelled as 'Junius Brutus' and formerly in the Palazzo Barberini). Here we see a noble Roman patrician or senator clad in his toga and carrying a pair of ancestral busts, one in each hand (the head of the senator himself is actually a restoration from another ancient statue). The statue probably dates from the end of the first century BC and it has been suggested that the family relationship represented is the senator-patrician with his father and grandfather. It is a pity that the original head of the statue has gone because a family likeness could well have been apparent. As it is, the portrait bust in the right hand seems to copy the style of the period of the mid-first century BC and the one in the left that of some 20 years later.

Previous page: In the relief processions of Imperial family, senators and priests on the sides of the Ara Pacis of Augustus the sculptor has cleverly intermingled the forms by having some turning back, heads looking over other people's shoulders, to give an excellent impression of both the participants and the actual slow moving procession.

Above: The statue of a senator holding two family portrait busts sums up the very essence of Roman formal portraiture at the end of the Republic. Palazzo dei Conservatori, Rome.

sentation of power. One of the most famous portraits of Augustus is the militarily attired statue found in his wife's (the empress Livia) villa at Prima Porta just outside Rome. It is slightly overlifesize and shows Augustus dressed as a Roman general holding a long staff in his left hand and raising his right hand in an outflung gesture. The stance is one which was to become very well known as the reverse type of a number of the large orichalcum (brass) coins called sestertii. The emperor is shown standing on a rostrum addressing troops gathered before him; it is referred to as an *ad locutio* scene, these actual words often appearing on the coin. The face is quiet but strong, the general in command of himself and his troops. He wears a highly ornamented cuirass, which in itself is not unusual but, being Augustus, his has deeper connotations with historical implications. Centrally placed is a barbarian in the act of handing a legionary standard to a legionary standing on the left, a dog at his feet. This scene refers

The style of the toga is Augustan so it would appear that we have three generations of the family spanning about 65 years. A point of technical interest is the use of the ornamented pillar or pseudo tree-stump that is cleverly used to provide a support for the right side of the statue which stands a little freer than the left side. In this example we see the epitome of the Roman portrait statue – the search for realism in a portrait bust, something that was unknown to the Greek world because it thought that a bust could not comprehend the whole, a concept that did not worry the Roman sculptor.

A similar realism is seen in a green basalt head of a man (misnamed 'Caesar') in the Museo Baracco. This has its antecedents in Late Period sculpture in Egypt, especially in the Boston 'Green Head' of *circa* 220–180 BC and the Berlin 'Green Head' (both are of green schist) of *circa* 100–50 BC. Both show powerful portraits of shaven-headed men, their skulls marvellously giving an impression of the underlying bone structure, and thoughtful, caring faces. The Baracco head follows the same tradition and, although found in Rome, is Egyptian work reflecting the realism of Ptolemaic Egypt and Republican Rome. It underlines how commissions would be placed for the use of a particular stone and the local traditions would still appear in the work; the veneer of Rome could at times be very thin.

At the beginning of the empire two statues of Augustus, the first emperor of Rome, present us with interesting studies in the religious and secular repre-

Above: Augustus as Pontifex Maximus (Chief High Priest) has an air of serenity in his features as he stands with toga drawn over his head to make sacrifice. Museo Nazionale, Rome.

Above left: A dark green basalt head of a man, probably a priest, found in Rome is Egyptian work and has kept the formal elements of Late Egyptian sculpture in hard stone but also suggested the formalism of Rome. Museo Baracco, Rome.

Above right: The military statue of Augustus from Livia's villa at Prima Porta is the forerunner of such genre representations that were to become the accepted norm under the Empire, in statuary and in the propaganda *Ad locutio* types on coins. Vatican Museums.

Right: The statue of Claudius represented as Jupiter is rather anachronistic, even his attendant eagle appears to look askance. Vatican Museums.

to the event in 20 BC when the disgrace of the battle of Carrhae in 53 BC (the Parthians had defeated the Roman army under Crassus, killed him and captured the standards) was mitigated by the return of the standards at the conclusion of a treaty. Personifications of the Sky and Sun are above while to the right and left are two prisoners, perhaps representing Spain and Gaul. Below the central group is a reclining female figure Mother Earth with a cornucopia and flanking her are Apollo and Diana. The symbolism of the statue does not stop there; it has been suggested that the little cupid balanced on a dolphin and steadying himself against the emperor's right leg is an allusion to his family, the Julian gens (clan), who were alleged to be descended from the goddess Venus via Aeneas, son of Anchises. The quest for realism and symbolism goes hand in hand with most statues that were produced for an official function.

The second statue of Augustus is later in date. He is shown in his office of Pontifex Maximus, High Priest, making sacrifice in the approved fashion with his toga draped over his head. His outstretched right hand would have held a patera (shallow dish, now missing, that was held in such rituals). The folds and drapery of the toga are quite well represented, but they are by a different sculptor from the one who carved the head and the right arm and left hand. These were separately carved and added to the statue, possibly because the original was damaged in some way and the body replaced. Although Augustus was now old, he was in his mid-60s, there is still a certain youthful air about the face although the hollow cheeks do indicate that age advances. Here, in the gentle, serene yet intense portrait there is a distinct contrast to the Prima Porta statue. They are virtually the same size statues of the same man, but they are poles apart, each in their own realization of Roman realism.

Having observed Augustus as general and high priest, it is interesting to look at just two other examples of imperial sculpture that see the emperor in a different guise. One is a statue of Claudius (AD 41–54) and the other of Commodus (AD 180–192). Claudius is represented as Jupiter wearing armor but has a wreath of oak leaves on his head; a medallion of an eagle with outstretched wings is at the front of the wreath. Although Claudius became emperor almost by accident, the Praetorian Guard seizing him and declaring him emperor after Caligula's murder, he was quite an able man, although inclined to be studious. His identification with the supreme god was not untoward since most emperors (except those whose memory was officially damned – *damnatio memoriae*) were deified after their death. This is a good portrait in the Augustan tradition that also scrupulously continues the typical Julio-Claudian hair style.

The second bust, beautifully preserved from the end of the second century AD, exhibits very fine workmanship that is rather lost on the character of the subject.

It shows Commodus, a couple of years before his assassination, in the guise of Hercules. Toward the end of his life he was the victim of politico-religious mania and was addicted to Hercules, dressing up as him and endeavoring to emulate his exploits in the arena. Here he wears the pelt of the Nemaean lion which Hercules slew in exactly the same way as Hercules wore it, its mask forming a head-dress. In his right hand is Hercules' knotted club and in his outstretched left, the golden apples of the Hesperides. One of a pair of kneeling Amazons at the base allude to Commodus' assumed name Amazonius. Although a masterpiece of sculpture as a portrait of the insane emperor, the sculptor has made the whole effect top heavy by too sudden a contrast between the muscular torso of the emperor and the way it is apparently insecurely balanced on the slender base of crossed cornucopiae and a globe.

Another contrast in imperial representations is the little group in red porphyry of the four Tetrarchs built into the outside corner of St Mark's, Venice. The two Augusti and the two Caesars, Diocletian and Maximian, Constantius and Galerius, are shown in full military battle dress and with the low 'pill box' hat of the Tetrarchic period. They embrace in friendly fashion, a gesture of solidarity, each with one hand on his eagle-headed sword. These statues at the end of the third century AD (Diocletian reigned AD 284–305) are a turning point from the world of Imperial Rome into the Late Antique world of Byzantium. In fact, they are almost medieval in their style and portraits of the emperors from this date to the fall of the empire in the West in 476 all tend to have similar, almost bland, features.

Portrait busts or statues of Roman ladies do not survive in such numbers as for men, obviously male representations were more appropriate in that society. Similarly, only ladies of high rank were portrayed and while it is possible to recognize most of the representations of the empresses, many others remain with a label that only places them within a given period. A great help in dating female sculpture are the hairstyles. As nowadays, there was a tendency to copy the style worn by the leading ladies. The portraits of the imperial ladies which appear on coins are especially important, and they can often be the deciding factor when ascribing a bust.

Like the statues of Augustus at the head of the imperial tradition, there is a female head in the Louvre that is similarly the beginning for that genre. Carved from basalt, a very hard Egyptian stone, it may well have been created in Egypt but it is certainly wholly in the Roman tradition. It is often called 'Octavia,' who was the sister of Augustus and married to the consul Marcellus. However, nowadays the general tendency is to identify the lady as Livia, the wife of Augustus. The profile view is especially closely paralleled by her representation on coins. A cameo in the Royal Coin

Left : This bust of Commodus, represented as Hercules with whom he identified himself in his madness, is very unbalanced and top heavy but the sculptor has produced a fine effect of the emperor, and especially of his luxuriant hair and beard, by clever use of the bow drill. Capitoline Museum, Rome.

Below : The small group of the four Tetrarchs built into a corner of St Mark's, Venice, dates from the late third/early fourth century AD but very much pre-empts the later, more bland, style of representation found in Late Antiquity. The hard red porphyry from Egypt was used sparingly for sculpture in the early empire but became commoner later, although its density did not lend itself well to portraiture.

Below left : The green hard stone head of the empress Livia reflects the same formalism of Roman sculpture found in the male busts. Note the very high smooth finish achieved by the sculptor. Louvre, Paris.

Right : A remarkable example of an Imperial lady's hairstyle in the early second century is seen in the bust of Vibia Matidia, Trajan's niece. It represents a *tour de force* by the sculptor and his bow drill. Capitoline Museum, Rome.

Above : The composed, almost severe, features of this portrait statue aptly reflect the honor and office of the unknown Vestal Virgin portrayed. Museo Nazionale, Rome.

Left : The marble head of Faustina II, wife of Marcus Aurelius, is a study in serenity of features and a pretty yet restrained hairstyle. H. Mahboubian Collection of Ancient Art.

Right : Sometimes in a piece of sculpture the Roman sculptor could go almost to extremes verging on the macabre in pursuing his aim of truth and accuracy. This wizened old toothless shepherdess is a fantastic study of face and bone structure. Museo dei Conservatori, Rome.

Cabinet in the Hague with a profile portrait to the left is very close, but then so also is another cameo in the Bibliothèque Nationale, Paris, labelled Octavia, with right-facing profile. Both ladies have similar hairstyles and features. The basalt bust dates to the last half of the first century BC, probably close to the date of the battle of Actium in 31 BC. There is a certain melancholy air about the face that is well brought out by the high degree of finish achieved in the hard basalt. Once again we see here the realism that the Roman sculptor aimed for; the resolute face and chin would have been subtly idealized in the earlier Greek tradition.

Two other imperial ladies of the early second century AD give us a contrast in the sculptor's approach. The first is usually identified as a bust of Vibia Matidia, who was the emperor Trajan's niece. The head is in the style of the Flavian period and probably dates around AD 98. As a representation of a lady's hairstyle this is a virtuoso piece. The tightly turned curls are piled high above her head with tremendous effect. Whoever the sculptor was, he was obviously a master of the use of the bow drill. The unusually high mass of curls contrasts heavily with the tight, almost dragged back hairstyle of Trajan's wife Plotina. A softer, face-framing effect is favored a few years later by Faustina II (daughter of Antoninus Pius and Faustina the Elder), who was the wife of Marcus Aurelius. The much sought-after realism is still here but perhaps the softer lines of the face are a reflection of her husband's philosophic nature.

On a par with the imperial ladies in terms of their social standing were the Vestal Virgins. While the former were the foremost ladies of the imperial court the latter were held in the highest regard by all. The small circular temple of Vesta in the Forum was the most important religious site because it was there that the priestesses guarded the sacred flame that symbolized the perpetuity of the State. It was ceremonially renewed every year on 1 March. Beside the temple was a spacious house, the home of the six Vestal Virgins, where important State as well as private documents such as wills were desposited. The Vestals were treated with great honor, as befitted their high rank. Statues of the chief Vestals stood on pedestals around an oblong pool in the atrium of their house (and several are still *in situ*). One of the finest statues (minus her hands and lower torso) shows a face expressive with concern and the sensibility of her high office. The drapes of her headdress and costume are carefully rendered with a discreet regard to the lady's person.

Pursuing the cult of realism the Roman sculptor at times seems almost to have gone too far, especially when representing older, working folk. An old shepherdess, her drapery falling open to reveal her wizened breasts and gaunt rib structure, can be seen to be literally stomping along with her long stick in one hand and a lamb clasped against her right thigh with the other. The details of old veined fingers and careworn face with its sunken cheeks and fallen mouth through loss of teeth is truly remarkable, almost repellent in a way. Other similar studies of old folk, such as an elderly fisherman or the old woman crouching holding a pottery drinking vessel, betray the sculptor's almost morbid fascination with portraying in excessive detail the hardship of the plebs.

At the other end of the spectrum from the old shepherdess, in complete contrast, is the so called Esquiline Venus, an extremely nubile young lady. A young girl or woman binding a fillet around her head (there are traces of one of her hands at the back of the head, although the arms are missing) was a favorite subject, part of the repertoire of Aphrodite (or Venus) after her bath. The realistic treatment that the sculptor has given to the lower torso and rather fleshy hips and legs leaves little doubt that this was modelled from life. Perhaps she was the teenage daughter of a Roman noble, or even his youthful wife, whom he wanted to immortalize in stone. The statue was found in 1874 in the Villa Palombara on the Esquiline, along with the bust of Commodus as Hercules. In the second and third centuries AD, it was not uncommon for the wealthier classes, who could afford to commission such sculpture, to decorate their large houses in this way. We find a somewhat podgy matron represented nude as Omphale, carrying her hard-won trophies of Hercules' lionskin and club, or another group, a couple from Ostia, with the husband shown as Mars being entreated by his wife as Venus, her drapery slipping but her hair neatly held in place by her stephane.

With the Roman sculptor ever striving after realism in portraits, it is quite refreshing at times to find expressions of his humanity in dealing with children and animals. Both together occur in a charming little group of a chubby naked infant wrestling with his pet goose. It is a subject that, while popular and frequently used for fountain decorations and the like, goes back much earlier. This example dates to the second century AD but its antecedents lie in a bronze group created by Boethus of Chalcedon in the second century BC. Another popular group motif was that of playful animals, unlike the often ferocious attacks portrayed in the mosaics. Several examples exist of a charming study of two hunting dogs squatting while one raises a paw to the other's shoulder and gently bites its ear. They show another side to the Roman character perhaps best described in the all-embracing French term as *sympathetique*.

Animals could also serve their turn in religious art and one of the most often repeated groups is the *tauromachia*, the bull-slaying Mithras. Originally a deity introduced from Persia, Mithraism was especially adopted by senior ranks in the army and wealthier merchants. Part of the myth structure dealt with the god Mithras slaying the bull in an underground cave. Pulling its head back by its dewlap, the Phrygian-capped god plunges his dagger into the bull's shoulder

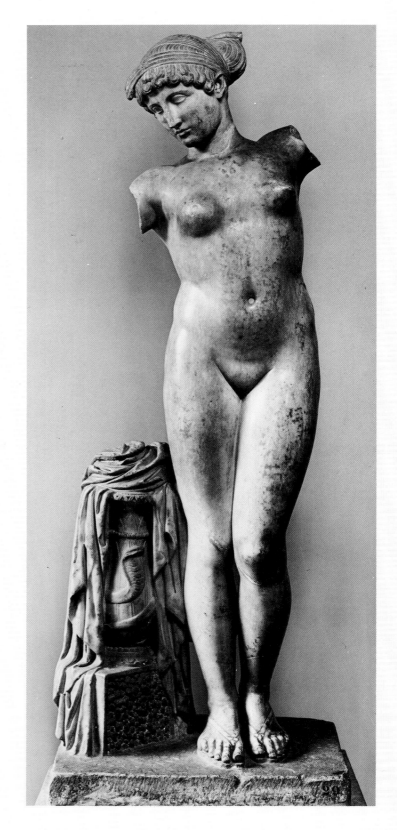

Above: In the Esquiline Venus a young Roman matron has been translated into the style but certainly not the form of the goddess for a patron who no doubt wished to please his wife with a statue of her taken from life. Capitoline Museum, Rome.

Right: The bull slaying of the god Mithras is a subject that occurs throughout the length and breadth of the Empire, usually as sculpture in the round or as stone or plaster reliefs. The basic elements of the god and the animals are always the same although the level of competency does vary. Louvre, Paris.

Left : A charming study of a young boy hugging his pet goose. Capitoline Museum, Rome.

Above : This group of two squatting dogs, one playfully nuzzling the other, is a basic representation that is known from several extant examples. It well demonstrates the Roman sculptor's affinity with animals. Vatican Museums.

and heart. A dog leaps to lick the blood and a snake moves up toward the wound. At the same time a scorpion attacks the bull's genitals. Both dog and snake seek the blood for its life-giving quality in order to be able to pass it on to mankind. Ears of corn were supposed to have sprung from the blood and the bull's tail. By this great feat Mithras gave benefit to mankind and the subject appeared on the back wall of every Mithraeum, either as a three-dimensional sculpture or as a carved relief in stone (even plaster at times) and could also be the main subject of a dedicatory plaque by an ardent worshipper. The subject appeared from one end of the Roman empire to the other, from as far as Dura-Europos in the east to Hadrian's Wall in the far north-west.

With relief sculpture the Roman artist/sculptor often had more latitude in the presentation of the subject. Three-dimensional sculpture was restricted because it was expensive, and was either commissioned by officials or by a wealthy patron. Reliefs could be and were commissioned by official sources, either for a religious function or perhaps as an historical commentary, such as Trajan's or Marcus Aurelius' Column. But there was other scope with reliefs, especially in the provision of funerary monuments, reliefs on tombs or the carving of scenes on sarcophagi. Here full rein could often be given, be it the depiction of episodes from myth and legend, battle scenes or even homely vignettes of daily life. It is particularly from the sarcophagi reliefs and funerary monuments that we can obtain most visual detail about many aspects of Roman daily life. A good way of observing Roman reliefs is to see them in

relation to their representations rather than solely through a clinical dissection of style.

At the head of Roman reliefs, bridging in its style the division between the Republic and Imperial Rome, stands the Altar of Augustus (the Ara Pacis) in the Campus Martius. Although strictly speaking it is an architectural monument, its reliefs are our prime interest. It was erected to mark Augustus' victorious return from Gaul and Spain in 13 BC and dedicated on 30 January, 9 BC. In late antiquity it gradually disappeared from view, sinking into the marshy depths where it stood close by the Tiber. Fragments of the reliefs were first found in 1568 when the Palazzo Peretti (now Fiano) was being built and then concentrated work in 1903 and especially in 1937/38 – when the ground had to be deep frozen about the remains in order to be able to extract them from the marsh – brought the rest to light. It was reconstructed from the original pieces recovered and casts but turned through 90 degrees when rebuilt so that it is now orientated roughly north-south when it was originally east-west. It takes the form of a walled precinct enclosing a central altar, the whole set on a podium with an external approach flight of steps at the original west (now south) end and another entrance at the east (now north) end. The interior altar has a frieze of reliefs of a ritual nature showing a procession of Vestal Virgins and animals for sacrifice on quite a small scale. The interior wall of the precinct is decorated with hanging swags above a wooden palisade effect. It is, however, the relief decoration on the exterior that makes the monument.

sides is a procession of a double row of figures clad in their official apparel, togas and wreaths. They must represent those who actually took part in the official procession at the inauguration, frozen in stone from a moment of time. There are the members of the Imperial family, with small children clutching their parents' hands or a hem of their gowns; senators, some serious, some turning to talk to a neighbor; priests carrying their ritual implements, jugs and shrines; and all the other officials necessary for such an important occasion. Although obviously a work of Roman sculpture and indeed very much a Roman subject there is an element in the carving that once again points outside Rome, perhaps to Hellenistic sculptors possibly using local sculptors of talent but nevertheless putting their stamp on the monument in little details like the juxtaposition of heads, the feet turning in different directions, the approach to representing the children. It is a work of quality that is typical in its treatment of the Augustan Age.

An interesting parallel of virtually contemporary date is the series of reliefs from the so-called Altar of Ahenobarbus, but which actually comes from the temple of Neptune built or restored by Domitius Ahenobarbus and which is shown on a silver denarius struck by him as moneyer in 42/41 BC. These reliefs also relate to a blend of myth and history, the marriage of Neptune and Amphitrite (now in Munich) and the sacrifice of the festival of the Souvetaurilia, with the ram and reluctant pig being led forward (now in the Louvre, Paris). Reliefs dealing with religious processions and sacrificial animals invariably show phenomenal detail. Also in the Louvre is a section of a relief of the early second century BC showing a bull being led to the sacrifice. In the foreground is the bull itself, virtually three-dimensional, his decorated horns and garlanded head standing well proud of the background.

All round the exterior wall of the precinct there is a deep panel of cleverly carved, intertwined foliage. Above this is a long series of figural reliefs. Curiously, although there seems to be a remarkable homogeneity about the reliefs, they are independent of the reliefs of the altar and have merely a symbolic relationship between themselves. On either side of the doorways at each end are large panels (now with some sections missing) which symbolize the founding of Rome; the discovery of the twins Romulus and Remus by the wolf, Aeneas making sacrifice, and so on. On the two longer

The bull is held by the band around his muzzle by a figure, his muscles and veins as he exerts pressure to hold the bull's head steady are marvellously represented in the stone. To the left, a musician playing double pipes has his instruments carved completely clear of the stone, just held in his fingers. In the background, forming a frame for the whole scene, are detailed representations of the ornate bronze doorways to two temples. A relief of a similar sacrificial subject shows Marcus Aurelius sacrificing before the temple of Jupiter Capitolinus (identified by its pedimental sculptures but shown with four columns instead of the necessary six). There is a very clever use of space in this composition with the idea of a jostle of people about the emperor in the foreground, the procession moving in from the left and the bull hanging its head forward by the flute player in the manner of an interested spectator. The whole scene is contained by the steadying architectural lines in the background. Other beautifully carved relief panels from a monument of Marcus Aurelius of AD 180–190 were built into the attic storey of the later Arch of Constantine and thus preserved. No doubt they appealed to Constantine because of their military flavor – they refer to events in the wars against the northern barbarians just prior to the triumph awarded in AD 176.

Without doubt the greatest Roman military relief is Trajan's Column which stands in his Forum, not far from his Markets. These were carved out of the hillside to the north and so formed a backcloth to the column. Originally the column was crowned by a statue of Trajan, but this was removed in 1587 in favor of a statue of St Peter that now tops it. The architect was Apollodorus of Damascus, who created a spiral frieze 650 feet long and three feet high rising up the column on eighteen drums of marble. The column itself is 100 Roman feet high (97 feet) and was dedicated in AD 113 to commemorate Trajan's conquest of the Dacians (now modern Romania). The scenes record in great detail the exploits and deeds of the two Dacian campaigns in AD 101–103 and 104–106 which culminated in the flight of the gallant Dacian chieftain, Decebalus, and his honorable suicide true to his creed when finally caught by the Roman cavalry. Although the reliefs are sympathetic to a noble enemy, the ultimate Roman military machine is portrayed as Decebalus' severed head is carried off on a large charger and presented before the troops prior to being sent on to Rome.

The breadth and concept of the reliefs, let alone their execution, is amazing. There are about 2500 figures carved on the column, ranging from Oceanus and Trajan himself (seen several times over and always in profile) through all the ranks and levels of the Roman army and their barbarian adversaries. Virtually every aspect of Roman army life is represented: the official parades; the fighting and the fatigues; building bridges and forts; cutting down timber; besieging an enemy

Left: Trajan's Column with its wonderful 650 feet long spiral frieze showing the Danubian campaigns dominates the Forum of Trajan at its foot.

Top: The Danubian river god watches as legionaries march from their fortress with standards and full kit. In the second register they are seen building a fortress whilst Trajan looks on.

The enormous amount of accurate detail showing virtually every aspect of Roman army life is a treasure house for the military student. Lowest reliefs at the base of Trajan's Column, Rome.

Above: A spirited attack by Dacians on a Roman fortress. Relief detail, Trajan's Column, Rome.

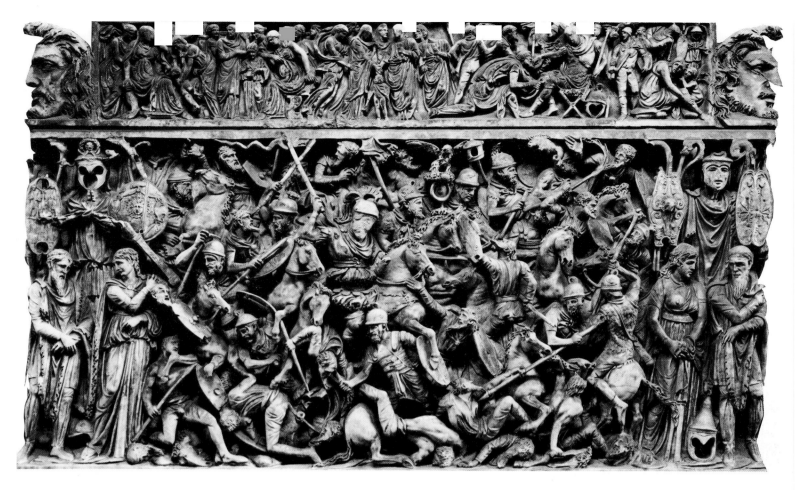

fort and in their turn being besieged; the attack in close order; the cavalry charge; the details of armored Sarmatian cavalry and the lightly clad Mauretanian cavalry on their lively steeds – there is never a dull moment or dull repetition of subject. Trajan's Column stands alone among Roman sculptural works – the Antonine Column, of Marcus Aurelius, is but a pale shadow beside it. As a historical record it is unique in its detail, its concept and its accuracy and is the premier example of Roman historical relief carving. Trajan's Dacian wars also found themselves a monument at Adamklissi (Romania) but the reliefs here were of local workmanship and are interesting by their very contrast in relating to the same subject. The great drum-like monument is now much denuded and the panel reliefs set around it in a broad circle.

The Roman sculptor's delight in detailed representation of lively military action is well seen in a number of sarcophagi that represent battles between Romans and barbarians (usually only on the front and premier panel). The type becomes very popular in the last quarter of the second century AD and obviously looks to both the columns just mentioned. A sarcophagus of truly intricate detail is in the Museo delle Terme, Rome, and probably belonged to a general of Marcus Aurelius who fought in the Germanic wars. The intricacy of the carving, with its interlocking of men and animals in a mad mêlée, shows a complete command of and confidence in the concept and, not least, in the bow drill to achieve such effects. Very noticeable are the individual

Above: The intricate detail of the carving on the Ludovisi sarcophagus showing a battle between Romans and barbarians. On the lid, a defeated chieftain kneels to kiss the emperor's (Marcus Aurelius) proffered hand. Of all the various faces depicted here the major one, that of the owner on horseback in the center of the melée, is unfinished. Museo delle Terme di Diocleziano, Rome.

Left: Tombstone of the centurion Marcus Favonius Facilis of the Twentieth Legion that was erected by two of his freedmen, Verecundus and Novicius. Colchester and Essex Museum, Colchester.

Below: The first-century AD tombstone of Rufus Sita, a Thracian cavalryman of the Sixth Cohort, shown riding down a barbarian foe is the earliest known example of this *genre* – it was to become extremely popular in the western provinces. Gloucester City Museum, Gloucester.

Bottom left: Relief carved in fine detail of members of the élite Praetorian Guard with their eagle standard. Capitoline Museum, Rome.

studies of grimacing Romans and, at the corners at either end, the despondent barbarian couples. Among all these facial studies (there are over 100 figures on the sarcophagus) one face has been left blank, the central horseman. No doubt the sculptor was awaiting a sitting or a likeness of the owner, but perhaps he needed the sarcophagus before it could be completed.

At the other end of the scale from the rough and tumble of the battle, were the emperor's élite corps, the Praetorian Guard on official duty in Rome (their nine cohorts of 500 men were stationed there). It was the equivalent of a cermonial regiment, but one that was a power in the land. Often it was solely instrumental in removing emperors as well as declaring them, out of sympathy as with Claudius, or for money as with Didius Julianus. Their level of pay, discipline and equipment was considerably above that of the ordinary legionary and the command was restricted to knights of the equestrian order.

Throughout the empire there are many monuments to soldiers of different classes and ranks and it is sometimes amazing how much information they can provide, quite apart from their artistic value. Over so wide a geographical area and time span there are obviously great differences to be seen, not least in the local sculptor's style and the financial commitment involved (usually borne by the heirs of the deceased commemorated). A tombstone in the Bonn Museum shows the centurion M Caelius, wearing the civic crown of oak leaves, awarded for saving the life of a citizen, and six *phalerae* (medals) plus torques and bracelets – all awards. He was killed with the three legions of Varus that were ambushed in the German forests in AD 9. An *aquilifer* (standard bearer) Gn. Musius of the XIV Legion *Gemina*, in Mainz, has similarly been awarded *phalerae*. One of the best-known reliefs of a centurion (and possibly the earliest surviving sculpture from Roman Britain) is that of M Favonius Facilis of the XX Legion (in Colchester). He stands quite calm and confident, gazing at the viewer, his vine stick of office in his right hand. The portrait, stance and general appearance of the monument all point to a sculptor of first-class ability who was trained in the Mediterranean. At the other end of the artistic scale are the reliefs cut from local stone by local sculptors which often have a splendor, vigor and immediacy, such as the tombstone of Rufus Sita, a Thracian cavalryman of the VI Cohort, seen riding down a barbarian, which came from Gloucester. On most of these tombstones the details would normally have been picked out in color, which has invariably long since disappeared.

Many aspects of Roman daily life can be seen in reliefs other than funerary sculpture. Shipping and trade was an important part of the Roman economy, not least the annual grain fleet which sailed from Alexandria in Egypt to Ostia, the port of Rome. A splendidly detailed relief of the early second century AD has a view of the busy harbor at Ostia, begun under

Claudius and completed by Nero (who featured a bird's eye view of it on one of his coins). A large merchantman puts into harbor, it sails decorated twice over with the wolf and twins motif; people bustle about on board and a carpenter is seen using an adze on a piece of timber. Behind it rises a triple-tiered pharos (lighthouse), based on the famous one at Alexandria, with flames issuing from the top. Another ship nearby (now damaged) has a large eye as a protective motif; men climb the rigging while others unload it, staggering under the weight of great sacks. Various deities are shown round about, also a quadriga (four) of elephants which is more normally a symbol of the deification of the emperor. A nude standing figure of Neptune, clasping his long trident, takes a benevolent view of the overall scene.

A third-century funerary monument, carved in high relief from Neumagen near Trier in Germany, shows a different kind of craft, a river boat with high prow and stern loaded with barrels of wine and quite a large crew in relation to the cargo. At Ravenna there is a tall tombstone of a shipbuilder which shows two pairs of conventional couples of the Longidieni family but at the bottom we see the shipwright himself, busy with adze, and the inscription records 'Publius Longidienus hastens to get on with his work.'

A very unusual relief from Epinal, France, shows a pharmacist in his workshop with his assistant working behind him with pestle and mortar. L Cornelius Atimento, who was an ironmonger by trade, had himself

Above: Relief showing the Trajanic port of Ostia with extensive detail and activity, all under the watchful eye of a large standing figure of Neptune. Galleria Torlonia, Rome.

Left: Finely carved sarcophagus fragment illustrating the use of horses to turn large mills for grinding corn. The complete sarcophagus must have been a very fine object and interesting because of its highly unusual choice of main subject. Vatican Museums.

Below: An unusual relief of a wine ship loaded with barrels of wine from Neumagen, near Trier, an area of Germany still noted for its light white wines. Landesmuseum, Trier.

Far right: Tomb relief commemorating P. Longidienus Camillus and his family and showing him hard at work on a ship's timbers using an adze. Museo Nazionale, Ravenna.

Right: Relief of the interior of a pharmacist's shop showing an assistant using a pestle and mortar in the preparation of soaps and salves. Such rare illustrations throw considerable light on various aspects of Roman daily life. Epinal Museum, Vosges.

EABR·NAVALIS·SE·VIVO·CONSIT
ET·LONCIDENAE·PISTACINI

P·LONCIDIENVS·P·ER·VFIO
P·LONCIDIENVS·P·L·PILADES·B
IN·PENSA·APRCNO·DEDERVNT

represented with a customer (or a relative?) in his shop with all his wares hanging up on his first-century tombstone. Another sarcophagus fragment shows horses being used to turn great stone querns to grind the corn (such querns can still be seen standing in baker's shops in the ruins of Pompeii today). Above the horses is a jolly scene of schoolboys at play, and there are a few girls as well on the left. The Igel monument near Trier (already mentioned) gives a valuable insight into a Roman household. While the Secondini family sit around a table at ease talking to each other the sculptor has shown the activity going on in other rooms, the preparation of the food in the kitchen, cleaning the dishes and selecting and decanting wine in the cellar. Although not often great works of art such reliefs are invaluable treasures because they allow us to see Roman life as it was and to be able to identify so many of the individuals concerned.

Highly placed officials would often prefer to extol their virtues or their office on their funerary monuments. A relief on a sarcophagus of the early second century AD (possibly from Ostia) shows a most important aspect of Roman life (after bread): the circus. It has a certain dignity about it, lacking the usual hurly-burly of so many sarcophagi reliefs of this type of scene where chariots rush pell-mell, crashing into each other, and excited spectators are shown in the background as officials turn down the dolphin-shaped lap markers. This is the monument of a magistrate (an *aedile*) who was responsible for the circus entertainment. His duties were obviously taken very seriously, one look at his face tells us that. Beside him a charioteer takes his four-horse team round, restraining the pulling horses. A youngster scatters something from a bowl, some kind of grip material perhaps, and the single horseman precedes them. In the background the structure of the circus building is quite well represented, albeit at an odd angle to get it to fit in. A winged cupid stands by

Top: The reliefs on the Igel Monument near Trier show the Secondini family seated around a table and interesting details of domestic servants at work in other rooms.

Above: The lugubrious face of the *aedile* (magistrate) on this sarcophagus relief from Ostia is in direct contrast to the animation of circus entertainment for which he was responsible and with which he chose to decorate his sarcophagus. Vatican Museums.

Right: A child's life from the cradle to a young scholar is represented in high relief on the sarcophagus of M. Cornelius Statius. Louvre, Paris.

the dolphin lap counters and in the center is a pyramidal obelisk set in the middle of the *spina* that divided the course down the center. The scene is probably set in the Circus Maximus and the central obelisk would be the one brought from Egypt in 10 BC and which now stands in the Piazza del Popolo, Rome. Circus racing scenes were not only popular as reliefs on sarcophagi, they frequently appear on pottery vases and oil lamps.

A different kind of chariot, a smaller version made up as a child's go-cart, appears in the center of the long side relief on the sarcophagus of M Cornelius Statius. It charmingly represents the development of a boy, seen

Below: Seated in her comfortable tall wickerwork chair a lady of Roman Germany has her hair attended to while her female servants fuss round her, one holding a mirror for her to observe the effect. Relief from Neumagen. Landesmuseum, Trier.

Right: The Apotheosis of Sabina, wife of Hadrian, showing her being carried heavenward on the back of a winged Victory who holds a long flaming torch. Such deification scenes for emperors, in relief or on coins, invariably show them being carried on the back of an eagle and empresses on a peacock. Capitoline Museum, Rome.

LIO·M·F·PAL·STATIO·P   ·FECER·

first at his mother's breast while his father looks on, then dandled by his father and next, older and bigger, driving his scaled-down chariot drawn by a family pet. Finally he presents himself, scroll in hand, before his schoolmaster who leans contemplatively on his hand. Another aspect of the household on a sarcophagus from Neumagen, Trier, has a homely scene of a Roman matron with her maids around her having her hair styled. Two seem to be concerned with the actual styling, a third holds a mirror so that she may watch them and a fourth (now mostly broken away) stood nearby holding a pitcher. An interesting detail is the Roman lady's chair with its elaborate basketwork. She seems quite at ease in it with her footstool before her.

By virtue of their nature sarcophagi reliefs are more concerned with death and life after death than with the aspects of daily life that we have been looking at. Among the most popular representations, because of the connotations of life after death and an enjoyment of that life, are those showing the triumph of Bacchus (Dionysus) and the Bacchic rout. Essentially the often highly active scenes show the god on his triumphant return from India surrounded by his attendants, satyrs and maenads, all making merry with music, song and dance. The subject owes much to pre-Roman art, to the Hellenistic world, but it is one which is found all over the empire although there is, as may be expected, rather more emphasis on those sarcophagi that come from the eastern provinces. Very fine examples exist in many major museum collections but a rather touching example is one that obviously doting and wealthy parents commissioned for their young daughter. It is carved on both sides, the front carrying an inscription set within a central panel on the lid. It translates as: 'To the memory of the sweetest daughter (*filiae dulcissimae*) Maconiana Severiana, her parents Marcus Sempronius Proculus, Vir Clarissimus, and Praecilia Severiana, Clarissima Femina [had this sarcophagus made].' The titles indicate that the parents were of senatorial rank, the young girl was of very good family. The date of the sarcophagus is early in the third century AD, about AD 210–220.

Merry rather than sad scenes might be expected on a child's sarcophagus, but here, on Maconiana's, we find

a full Dionysiac panoply on the front. The god himself stands in the center, perhaps a little tipsy, supported by a satyr while an ecstatic maenad dances to the music of her tambourine on his other side. All around are Bacchanalian figures but Dionysus' gaze is turned toward a wild satyr on the right who is drawing back a drapery to reveal a nude sleeping Ariadne. The scene is part of the legend when, Theseus having abandoned Ariadne on the isle of Naxos as he returned to Athens after slaying the Minotaur in Crete, Dionysus and his followers found her asleep on the island. The god fell in love with Ariadne and married her. The overtones are all of joy in the next world for the young girl making her way there. On the back panel is a scene of vintaging and grape treading, a popular image right into Christian times where it appears on the red porphyry sarcophagus of Constantine the Great's daughter, Constantia.

Also extremely popular as sarcophagi reliefs were scenes from Homer's *Iliad*, and they do not seem to discriminate too much between the two sides, Trojans and Greeks, so long as the fate to be shown was a good one in illustrative terms. One favorite episode is where Odysseus tricks Achilles into revealing himself. Thetis, Achilles' mother, had dressed him as a girl and hidden him among the daughters of Lycomedes in an endeavor to stop him taking part in the Trojan War. The wily Odysseus threw down some weapons before the girls, knowing full well that one of them would not be able to resist handling them, and give himself away. A particularly fine relief of this moment is on an early third century AD sarcophagus in Rome. Achilles stands on the right, brandishing a sword while his woman's dress slips off him. One of the daughters, Deidamia, lays a restraining hand on his shoulder while her father, Lycomedes, watches seated on a low throne to the left. Wily Odysseus, well pleased with the success of his

strategem, stands at the extreme right beside the tall chair reserved for guests. Another interesting feature of this sarcophagus is its lid with the two reclining male and female figures. They conform more to the earlier tradition of Etruscan sarcophagi, with their couples molded in terracotta, than to the Roman tradition. Their drapery and languid pose also has links with the eastern empire, very reminiscent of contemporary Palmyrene reliefs in the area of Syria. A legend connected with this sarcophagus, which was found in 1582 in the Monte del Grano, just outside the Porta S Giovanni, is that the ashes of the two deceased were found in the sarcophagus in a decorated glass vase. It went to the Barberini collection and subsequently to the British Museum, where the 'glass vase' is better

known as the Portland Vase. However there is no real evidence for this.

The story of Troy continues on this sarcophagus on both the ends and the rear side (most unusually since often the back was left plain). One of the next major episodes is beautifully carved on a large sarcophagus in Providence, Rhode Island. This was cut in a workshop in Asia Minor about AD 190 and shows the victorious Achilles dragging the body of the Trojan Hector, whom he has just slain, around the walls of Troy as an object lesson to the Trojans. This episode is one which does no credit to the Greek hero. The sequel to this event, again quite popular, is a scene full of pathos; the old king of Troy, Priam, is on his knees pleading with Achilles for the return of the mangled body of his son, Hector, to give it decent burial. In most reliefs of this scene Achilles has his face averted in a distasteful manner.

With the wider acceptance of Christianity and its final authorization by Constantine in AD 313 the reliefs change, the old legends disappear and the new Savior, or biblical episodes, predominate. One of the earliest Christian sarcophagi (found in Rome and now in the Louvre) of third-century AD date follows the style of

Left : Achilles discovered, disguised among the daughters of King Lycomedes. Agamemnon, seated right with Odysseus standing beside him, watches as Achilles cannot resist the lure of weapons and gives himself away. Capitoline Museum, Rome.

Below and below left : The aged Priam, King of Troy, kneels to kiss the hand of Achilles (below), beseeching the return of the mangled body of his son Hector slain by Achilles and dragged behind his chariot around the walls of Troy (below left) in revenge for the death of his friend Patroclus. Louvre, Paris.

later pagan types in its 'bath tub' shape and ornamental strigils on the side, but it is the first of a long line of representations of Christ as the Good Shepherd, carrying the lamb over his shoulders. The lions' head masks, indeed the figure itself, are all rather Hellenistic in their style although still typical of the Roman carvers' workshops. More usual are scenes of Christ with the Apostles which tend to appear in the fourth century and later and, once again, while the basic subject matter of a central figure of Our Lord, attended on either side, is repeated, the treatment of faces and clothing is very indicative in many instances of the source of the piece.

Christian symbolism is to be expected on the great fourth-century red stone porphyry sarcophagi of the ladies of the House of Constantine but there is a degree of anachronism there. That of Constantine's mother, St Helena, is carved with Roman cavalry, barbarian prisoners and fallen warriors – in all probability it was intended for Constantine himself rather than St Helena. His daughter Constantia's sarcophagus was found in the family mausoleum of St Constantia. Although it has Christian imagery carved in the hard stone in high relief – erotes gathering grapes, a peacock, a ram and so on – many of these Christian symbols derive from pagan symbols. Particularly evident is the grape treading scene on one of the end panels; the whole vintage aspect is redolent of Bacchic origins but it has been made acceptable to the new, and now official, religion.

Roman reliefs can tell us much more about Rome and its way of life throughout the empire than sculpture can. The quantifying factor rests with the sculptor or craftsman responsible, his expertise as well as his flair in interpreting what his client wanted. Sometimes quite small details can open very wide doors of understanding.

Below: Christ as a teacher surrounded by the Twelve Apostles and others carved on a fourth-century sarcophagus found at Rignieux-le-Franc (Ain). Louvre, Paris.

Right: Christ seen as the Good Shepherd on a third-century sarcophagus, one of the earliest Christian sarcophagi with this iconography. Louvre, Paris.

6. Minor Sculptural Works

While architecture and sculpture (be it in the round or reliefs) invariably make an immediate if not overwhelming impression on the observer, many of the details associated with them are often lost in the view of the mass. Stuccowork is very much a case in point in this context. It seems to date from the first century BC in Italy and subsequently spread outward from there, rather like the ripples in a pool. Although examples of the craft are known from elsewhere in the empire it is to Italy that we must look for the best remaining examples. Once again, environmental factors determine the survival of the material; stuccowork has little chance of surviving in the damp northern provinces of the empire.

First, a word about the manufacture of stucco, then its use and motifs. As may be expected, both Vitruvius in his books on architecture and Pliny in his *Natural History* (which covers much else besides) give a lot of detail. Lime was the principal ingredient for the plaster and it is to be regretted that one of the best sources is from the burning of marble – many an ancient statue disappeared in medieval and later times into the ever-hungry lime-kilns. Limestone and chalk also produce lime. The burned material becomes quicklime; and water is added together with various binding agents which assist the molding capacity of the product and give it body. River sand and marble dust are the ingredients approved by Vitruvius. It was essential to produce a plaster that was of good color, reasonable consistency to take such molding as might be required but also, in its firmness, to be slow drying to allow for manipulation. Laying the plaster was a highly skilled job, as nowadays, and much the same implements were used, essentially the plasterer's float which was a flat board with a handle fixed to the back, and the round-ended trowel, the blade set at a sharp downward right-angle to the handle.

For a good job several layers, all properly finished, would be called for – Pliny suggests five, alternating sand-mortar and marble-stucco. This gives a good solid finish which can either be left plain and painted or, in its final stage, highly embellished by molded decoration. Upper walls and vaults were favorite areas for the application of stuccowork, sometimes repetitious geometric patterns were used with areas picked out in color, at other times the work was so complicated, with delicate moldings involving figures, that they can become minor works of art. Figures that were required to be in high relief often had a core protruding from the wall around which they could be built up. While molds would have been used to produce the major elements of the figures, there is little evidence of multiple repetition and so the presumption is that a large amount of hand finishing in the malleable plaster was carried out. It would certainly be a good explanation for the freshness of line and presentation observed in so much of the stuccowork that survives.

Stuccowork is found in private houses and also in temples, tombs and the catacombs. The temple of the Egyptian goddess Isis at Pompeii produced some fine stuccowork with figures from the little megaron (a ritual abluting area) just within the temenos and before worshippers turned toward the temple. In the house of a priestess of Isis (as it is often identified) near the Farnesina in Rome a remarkably delicate series of landscapes executed in stucco was found on the vaulting dating to the first quarter of the first century AD. A series of panels show houses and figures set in a landscape that exhibits great skill on the part of the plasterer. The houses are of many different kinds, some with tall tower-like structures closer to types found in later North African mosaics, others are just simple little loggias. They are cleverly represented as being seen from various angles, one pair even have a small curved bridge connecting them that is very reminiscent of the much later and well-known Willow Pattern plates with the small figures crossing the bridge and the delicately 'drawn' trees and their foliage.

This delicacy is lost later on in the first and then into the second century AD. Color applied to the flat backgrounds, leaving the modelled figures in white, becomes very garish and the figures do not have the same spon-

Left: Very fine and delicate stuccowork is a typical product of the early Imperial period, as here from the Augustan Farnessina villa with its fine landscape with figures. Museo Nazionale, Rome.

Below left: Several of the family mausoleums found in the upper levels of the catacombs along the Via Appia outside Rome have extensive areas of stuccowork with molded decoration on their vaulted ceilings as here in the San Sebastian catacombs.

Above: A remarkable piece of stuccowork sculpture was excavated in the tomb of the Valerii beneath St. Peter's, Rome. This head of a woman holding the edge of her veil is a magnificent facial study. Vatican Museums.

Previous spread: Polychrome stucco work in the Tomb of the Anicii, Via Latina, Rome, with figures in relief of three of the heroes from the Trojan Cycle, Patroclus, Achilles and Hector.

taneity. In the tomb of the Pancratii, a burial college (that is, religious undertakers) on the Via Latina in Rome, the decoration surrounding the central panel scenes has become very repetitive and even the central panels, with apparently quite animated gods and their attendants, lack the verve of the earlier products. Motifs are often similar to those found in reliefs and on the sarcophagi, especially relating to Dionysus and the Heavenly Twins, the Dioscuri, and others. Fine tracery and foliage decoration occur in the vaults of some of the better class tombs in the catacombs, such as at S Sebastiano on the Appian Way. An unusual use of stucco as a creative molding medium was found in the mausoleum of the Valerii excavated under St Peter's, Rome. The Valerii were adherents of the cult of Isis; a stucco figure of Apollo-Harpokrates (the latter the son of Isis) stands in a niche as the central figure of the north wall and a little girl has the lock of Isis at the back of her head. Unusually, the mausoleum is decorated overall with stuccowork instead of painting and it is interesting to note the scratched graffito head of St Peter, put there when the mausoleums in the area were closed under Constantine in the fourth century. Two broken marble portrait busts and a child's head in gilded marble were found there but it is the beautiful stucco head of a woman th... ...attention. It dates from the m...d second... ...(about two thirds lifesize. T...e lady... ...clothes with its drapery, held ...ghtly in her... ...fully rendered but it is the ...face... ...t has a restrained beauty, a... ...nose and mouth and, above all, an exp... ...of noble sorrow that is poignant in its intensity.

While Roman stuccowork was quite alive in its techniques and modelling, terracottas, which are not so far removed, failed to enjoy the popularity and appeal that they had in the Greek world. In ancient Greece terracotta modelling had reached great heights, in the Roman world it was essentially mundane by comparison. Stuccowork shows Hellenistic influences, terracottas do not. They are invariably mold-made, often with the second half, the back, being very roughly, if at all, modelled. In northern Europe pipeclay was widely used, generally to manufacture the little white pipeclay votive figurines of nude Venuses with elaborate hairdos. In the North African provinces a much wider repertoire of figures and animals was produced, some in quite good style and often highly colored. Subjects range across figures from legend to momentary vignettes taken from the ever-popular circus. Along the North African coast in Egypt there is a very distinctive school of terracotta manufacture, usually embellished with a plain red slip overall or with a white lime coating having bright color added. Favorite subjects, and very repetitive, are the young god Harpokrates in various attitudes, goddesses such as Isis or Demeter (the corn goddess, very popular as Egypt was the granary of Rome) and fashionable ladies with the most elaborate bouffant hairstyles; these often have large piercings in the earlobes which may have held earrings. Some of the finer work represents sporting activities such as a pair of wrestlers, or gladiators in combat.

The eastern Mediterranean Roman terracottas, and also those of Greece and Asia Minor, simply tend to carry on without too much notice of Rome. Old motifs and figure types continue to appear and, invariably, where figures are signed they are still signed in Greek.

There are some objects that survive which are difficult to categorize, yet they were highly prized in ancient Rome and are excessively rare survivals today. Such a piece is the Crawford Cup in the British Museum. It is a small drinking cup of kantharos shape, made of fluorspar which came from the Persian Gulf. Quite soft to work, it was rarely found in pieces large enough to work into a useful shape. The attraction lay not only in its rarity but in its coloring; it is translucent and has delicate shading in its wreathed veins through the violet and purple ranges of color. Cups made of this material were highly prized in antiquity. Pliny tells us how the emperor Nero paid 1,000,000 sesterces for a single cup made of it – that is about 2500 ounces of gold (approximately $600,000). He also tells of a Consul who owned a cup of fluorspar ('murrhine') and 'grew so

Above: One of the finest representational ivories to survive is this leaf from an ivory diptych of *c* AD 400 showing the Vandal chieftain Stilicho. Cathedral Treasury, Monza.

Top far right: The Crawford Cup, British Museum, London.

Top right, center and right: Roman terracottas never achieved the variety and skill in modelling that is evident among Greek terracottas. For once the Romans did not copy earlier styles, possibly because there was not the same interest in producing and using terracotta figurines. These examples, from different parts of the empire

exemplify this. From North Africa two pieces illustrate mythological subjects, the triumph of Dionysus with a young follower merrily playing double pipes while riding a panther, and Leda being carried off on the back of the swan (Zeus in disguise). From Macedonia comes an appealing, tightly cloaked, figurine of Telesphorus, Aesculapius' young companion and healing god. Terracotta figurines from Roman Egypt became very repetitious with many varieties of the young god Harpokrates. A very unusual representation is this young lady who raises her skirts to expose herself. Private collections.

passionately fond of it, as to gnaw its edges even' (it was quite soft). So valuable an item, if broken, could not be thrown away. He says, 'I saw counted the broken fragments of a single cup, which it was thought proper to preserve in an urn and display, I suppose, with the view of exciting the sorrows of the world, and of exposing the cruelty of fortune; just as though it had been no less than the body of Alexander the Great himself!'

Ivory was another material that had been widely used in ancient Greece right back into Minoan and Mycenaean times; a lot of the earlier pieces were made from the ivory of the Syrian elephant which became extinct about the ninth century BC. Later supplies had to be sought in North Africa, the Sudan and India. Few Roman ivories survive, except for the occasional small statuette which might be a human or animal study. It is really in the world of late antiquity, the Roman/Byzantine borders, that ivory working returns to any large degree. Mostly represented by carved leaves of diptychs of the sixth century and later, they still, curiously, embody a great amount of pagan iconography in their designs. A particularly interesting, early and historically important piece of carving, the wing of an ivory diptych of *circa* AD 400, just falls within our period. It shows the standing figure of the Vandal Chief, Stilicho, who virtually ruled the western Roman empire as regent for Honorius at the turn of the fourth and fifth centuries. While many of the representations of the imperial family, consuls, religious scenes and so on, on the later diptychs are often naive in their presentation and not of particularly good craftsmanship, this piece is outstanding. The ivory carver has completely captured the man, the strong face is framed by the carefully presented hair and close-cut beard. The stance and the details of Stilicho's dress and weapons, his oval shield and tall spear all project an impression of strength. It must count as one of the most important visual documents and representations to have survived from the last years of the waning Roman empire.

7. The Metalworker's Art

From Herculaneum this study of a pig leaping forward balanced only on its hind trotters is a highly unusual, as well as amusing piece. Museo Nazionale, Naples.

Metal, be it precious – gold, silver or electrum (a natural alloy of gold and silver) – or bronze, copper or lead, was always highly prized in antiquity. The ratios of value could change considerably, dependent on the sources of supply. Athens and Macedonia were both rich in silver (the latter also in gold) but, for example, in Egypt before Alexander the Great, silver was at a higher premium than gold because gold was common and silver virtually nonexistent. Metal was always easily reusable, be it a silver plate that had been damaged or a simple workman's chisel that had broken or become too blunted, so metal was never thrown away or abandoned in the way that other materials might be. Objects made of precious metals survive because they have either been overwhelmed by catastrophe such as the AD 79 eruption of Vesuvius, or they were hidden deliberately with intent to recover, either by their rightful owner at a time of stress or by a thief in a hurry, or they were buried with no intent to recover, that is, they were part of a funeral offering. From these several contexts it is quite amazing how much precious metalwork has survived from Roman times.

There were obviously certain local styles to be found in metalworking throughout the empire but it is very noticeable how much similarity there is in Roman silver plate from one end of the empire to the other, and this applies over a chronological as well as a geographical span. Basic forms continue, the decoration is much the same in its choice of iconography and, curiously, even the old pagan imagery continues to appear after Constantine the Great (as can also be seen in some relief sculpture and sarcophagi) and continues well into the early years of Byzantium.

Silver plate was not at all common until the second century BC. Rome's earliest coinage had reflected this scarcity in its large bronze bars and weighty coins; silver denarii, the denomination that was to become almost as stable as the later English silver penny (which derived its normal abbreviation 'd' from the denarius), were only introduced about 211 BC. There is hardly any silver plate which survives from the early Republic.

The turning point came with the Second Punic War. It opened the doors to the rich silver mines of Spain, long exploited by the Carthaginians and Phoenicians, and also Rome was able to 'acquire' large amounts of both gold and silver from southern Italy. There, in Magna Graecia, the Greek colonies were very rich from their motherland connections. Once they began to fall to the might of Rome, the booty flowed north to the city on the Tiber. Individuals, consuls, generals and the like began to acquire silver, both plate and by weight. Silver begins to appear much more in the literary references as it became the fashion for noble families to own and collect plate. Some were more unscrupulous than others, especially when they had the opportunity through holding high office. Cicero, in his prosecution of the praetor Verres in 70 BC for misuse of office and extortion while propraetor of Sicily in 73–71 BC, lists all sorts of statues, works of art and extensive collections of silver plate. The silver tongue of Cicero, the greatest prosecuting lawyer of his day, marks out Verres as one of history's greatest villains. Cicero said that Verres even went so far as to set up his own silversmithing factory so that his craftsmen could remount onto silver plates the *emblemata* (silver medallions) that he had squeezed out of or stolen from rich provincials. It is an interesting comment in light of such *emblemata* plates found in the villa at Boscoreale and the Hildesheim treasure. Silversmiths in Rome formed themselves into a guild and also had their own silver market, the *basilica argentaria*. As craftsmen whose expertise was highly valued by rich patrons they could and did move freely about the empire to where commissions called them or where they wished to set up their workshops.

Once quantities of silver were available silver plate became of the highest importance in the political, economic and domestic life of the empire. Every family of any standing had its collection of plate for domestic use as well as its showpieces that were family heirlooms. We can get a very good idea of what would be appropriate to a reasonably wealthy middle-class Roman family of the first century AD from a wall painting still *in situ* in the tomb of C Vestorius Priscus at Pompeii. It shows a silver dinner service (or part of one, there are no plates) where there are obviously 'sets': deep wine cups of kantharos shape in pairs; a pair of shallow stemmed *kylikes* (also for wine), of long ladles, of tall-footed and necked ewers and four small ladles. What we see represented is presumably a small side table from which servants would bring the requisite items to the main table as necessary. Any family lacking such tableware were looked upon with disdain as absolute paupers. Suetonius makes this point in his life of the emperor Domitian in *The Twelve Caesars*: 'Most people agree that Domitian spent a poverty-stricken and rather degraded youth: without even any silver on the family table.'

The earliest large collections of silver plate found date to the first century AD, the groups found buried in the eruption of AD 79 that struck down not only the well-known cities of Pompeii and Herculaneum but also many other smaller towns, like Stabiae, and large villas, like Oplontis, that lay around the Bay of Naples. The first of these large finds was made at the villa at Boscoreale two miles northwest of Pompeii in 1895. It consisted of 109 pieces of silver, over 1000 gold aurei and some jewellery. Nearby lay the skeleton of a woman, whether the lady of the house who had just cached her jewellery or some other person we do not know. The owner of the house perished in the lava flood and the tableware was never reclaimed. Most of the silver plate dates to the early part of the first century AD but one interesting piece was obviously a

Above: The imagery that the silversmith worked into the principal *emblema* dish from the Boscoreale treasure is not fully explained. The essential subject is the personification of Africa with various associated attributes but it must have meant something to the owners who commissioned such a work of art that could only be used for display purposes. Louvre, Paris.

family heirloom or collector's item because it was about 300 years older than the other items. It is a shallow silver *kylix* (wine cup) with wishbone handles and a design in the interior bowl of engraved lotus flower palmettes. It was made by a Greek craftsman working in South Italy about 300 BC and some letters found scratched among the floral decoration may indicate his name. This piece of silver plate is among the earliest found at Pompeii. The household silver was of various kinds, some were pieces for everyday use, others merely for display on a side table and there were also some toilet mirrors.

The most important pieces were the *emblema* dishes or bowls, large pieces with interesting raised central decorations. These were for ostentatious display since they would have been of little practical use. The major piece is perhaps one of the most important and interesting of its kind to survive – looking at it we can well understand Verres' lust for such pieces rather than sympathize with Cicero's condemnation of him for it. Rising in high relief from the center of the dish in silver gilt is the bust of a woman who has been variously identified as a personification of Africa, as Cleopatra VII and as the goddess Isis. The first is more probably correct because of the many different attributes that surround the figure. She wears an elephant headdress, the elephant's trunk rising above her brow and the tusks on either side; in her left hand is a cornucopia (horn of plenty) topped by a crescent moon and in her right hand

125

she holds an erect uraeus (the sacred cobra of ancient Egypt). A heavily maned lion crouches on her right shoulder and a female panther looks across at him from beside the cornucopia. Other noticeable motifs are the sacred sistrum (rattle) of Isis below the lion, a lyre, wheat, grapes and, below the bust, a small dolphin, a pair of pincers, a snake twined around a stick and what looks to be some kind of marker or *gnomen* with a domed top. The piece probably dates to the first century BC and is truly remarkable; it must have been quite stunning properly displayed among other, no doubt plainer, silver in the setting of the villa. Very interestingly the dish carries an inscription underneath that gives its weight overall and that of the *emblema* separately. It reads: *Phi*[ala] *et emb*[lema] *p*[endentia] *p*[ondo] 11 (= 2 librae) s = = (= dextans) > VI (= 6 scripula); *phi*[ala] *p*[endens] *p*[ondo] 11 (= 2 librae) = (= sextans) Σ (= ½ uncia); *emb*[lema] *p*[endens] *p*[ondo] s — (= septunx) Σ (= ½ uncia). It is not unusual to find weights scratched on pieces but strange that the two elements of the dish and its *emblema* should have been so carefully weighed separately. At a dinner party given by the wealthy Trimalchio, as recounted in Petronius' *Satyricon*, an ass made of Corinthian bronze stood on the dining table and 'carried two dishes engraved on the rims with Trimalchio's name and the weight of the silver.' This is typical of Trimalchio's ostentation in everything.

At least two other *emblema* dishes were among the hoard but only one of them survives complete. They were probably a matching pair. The survivor has the head of an elderly man rising in high relief from the central tondo. The style is Augustan and it may be presumed that the man represented was the father of the owner of the villa. Scratched on the underside is a graffito, *Maximae* (Maxima's) which was probably done by the owner of the dish. A silver head of a lady with a hairstyle that indicates an early first century AD date had become detached from the dish (now lost) and she was, presumably, the wife and pair to the elderly man dish.

There were a number of deep, two-handled *skyphoi* (drinking cups) among the group, several provided in pairs, decorated with splendid high-relief scenes in repoussé. Such cups were formed in at least two parts, usually more. The outer repoussé decoration would be highly finished with its figured scene but the interior, incuse, version would be left having an uneven surface. This would be concealed by a smooth inner lining being fitted into the cup and the two parts, or skins, would be soldered together around the rim. Handles and often a base ring foot would be added separately. Among the repoussé *skyphoi* from Boscoreale are a pair that show on one side a squatting boar amid all sorts of things such as flowers, turnips, a curved knife and a three-legged table, and on the other a mixed scene with a goose rushing at a dead hare suspended from a pole, a basket of shrimps, grapes and a couple of dead thrushes.

The cup is signed in Greek capital letters CABEINOC. He was probably the silversmith and, such were the pretensions of the period, he had to sign in Greek while his name was probably simply Sabinus. Other *skyphoi* of the same shape show an animated scene of a ferocious lion pacing right with forepaw raised and being 'steered' by a winged cherub on his back who firmly grasps his mane. Riding postillion behind the cherub is a youthful figure of Dionysus, leaning back to hurl a beribboned *thyrsus* (a wand, rather than a spear). In front of the lion is another cherub blowing merrily on a flute, an overturned goblet at his feet, and his matching companion behind the lion dances along hanging on to the lion's tail, having dropped his pan pipes on the ground. A pair of very elegant stemmed cups with high handles have charming representations of storks' nests on them.

A more sober but nevertheless most attractive decoration on another cup of the same shape has a branch of olives and leaves circling it. The berries are in very high relief and since they are almost in the round they had to be filled with lead to make them suitably robust. Where the stems stand proud, they

Left : The second silver *emblema* dish from Boscoreale probably shows a portrait of an ancestor of the owner and was a pair with a lady's head of similar style but for which no dish survived. Louvre, Paris.

Right : A fine two-handled silver cup from a drinking set with a spirited scene in high relief of a young Dionysus, a lion and cupid companions. Boscoreale treasure. Louvre, Paris.

Below : Silver two-handled and footed cup from the Boscoreale treasure. Louvre, Paris.

Below left : On this silver drinking cup olive berries stand out in such high relief that the cup could only have been used with great care to prevent accidental damage. Boscoreale treasure. Louvre, Paris.

127

Above: An unusually macabre representation of skeletons decorates this silver cup from the Boscoreale treasure. Louvre, Paris.

were cast separately and then soldered on. A cup with similar-style olive decoration was found in the House of Menander at Pompeii in December 1930. It stands on a low foot and has very elegant upturned handles which were only attached at the lower end. This was the second large hoard of Campanian silver. It comprised 118 pieces of silver tableware which had been carefully wrapped in cloth and stored in a bronze-bound wooden chest in the cellar of the house.

A pair of differently shaped cups from Boscoreale, tall beaker-like pieces with single handles and a flat foot that are probably the *modiolus* shape that appear in the texts, have a very odd scene in repoussé. It shows a *danse macabre* of skeletons, adults and children, engaged in various pursuits. Captions in Greek actually identify some of them as famous names, such as the two philosophers Zeno and Epicurus apparently engaged in a bitter argument. Above all their heads/skulls runs a high relief garland of fruits and leaves. These two cups are probably also earlier than the main hoard. They are certainly more Hellenistic if not eastern Roman in style.

Among all the other pieces of silver from the Boscoreale villa one last piece calls for comment since it is not a piece of tableware, either for use or display. It is a large silver hand mirror (almost one foot long overall). Its elegant alabaster handle supports a large dish which has, on its back, an ovolo molding around the rim and in the center an appliqué medallion with traces of gilding. The scene shows the lightly draped figure of Leda, daughter of king Thestius of Pleuron and wife of Tyndarus, king of Sparta, seated on a rock and feeding a swan out of a *patera* (shallow dish). Little does she realize here that the swan is Jupiter in disguise whose intentions toward her are less than honorable. Leda and the Swan is among the most popular motifs of antiquity (frequently appearing on the *discus* of oil lamps), in the Renaissance and later. The image of a woman being

embraced by a swan was a subtle form of eroticism that was acceptable when others might not have been. In the legend, as the outcome of this dalliance, Leda produced a series of semidivine children hatched from eggs that included the Dioscuri (the twins Castor and Pollux) and also Helen. Such richly styled mirrors have been associated by Pliny with the name of Pasiteles, a supreme craftsman in Magna Graecia (South Italy) in the mid-first century BC.

A number of pieces of silver plate of the Augustan period found their way via trade to points far beyond the Roman *limes* (frontiers). Mediterranean wine was much esteemed among the 'barbarian' chiefs of north-west Europe and amphorae (large wine jars) have been found in several of their graves. The appropriate drinking vessels, no doubt the better to savor the wine as well as for ostentatious display, accompanied the wine north and then accompanied their owners to the next world. Tacitus refers in his *Germania* (5) to Germanic chieftains and says, 'One may see among them silver vessels, which have been given as presents to their

Above left: On the back of a hand mirror from the Boscoreale treasure is shown a favorite motif of the classical world. Leda and the Swan. Louvre, Paris.

Left: Why a silversmith working in late Roman Gaul should produce a small silver bowl imitating glasswork is a mystery. Even more so is the fact that it then made its way to Haagerup, Fynen, in Denmark where it was found. Nationalmuseet, Copenhagen.

Below: On a fine silver drinking cup of the Augustan period found in a grave at Hoby, Denmark, far beyond the Roman frontiers, is represented a favorite scene from the story of Troy. Priam is seen kneeling to kiss the hand of Achilles who has slain his son Hector. The old king supplicates for the return of the body for decent burial. This same moment is also found on sarcophagi reliefs and in wallpaintings. Nationalmuseet, Copenhagen.

envoys and chiefs, as lightly esteemed as earthenware. The Germans nearest to us do, however, value gold and silver for their use in trade, and recognize and prefer certain types of Roman money.' The cups were generally provided in pairs, a fine pair with shapes like that from the House of Menander but not so simple and without the repoussé decoration, were found in a chieftain's burial at Welwyn, Hertfordshire, in 1906 (another, badly damaged, and presumably one of a pair, was excavated not far away at Welwyn Garden City in 1965). A splendid pair of decorated silver cups was found, along with a magnificent table service largely of fine bronzework, at Hoby, on the island of Laaland, Denmark, in 1920. Accompanying the dead chieftain to the grave were all the provisions he would need for the next world, including two joints of pork, the two silver cups already referred to placed on a tinned-bronze tray, a silver ladle, a bronze *situla* (bucket), jug, saucepan, drinking horns, brooches, rings, a belt-buckle and knife, as well as three pots. The two cups were of the same shape as the cupid and lion cup from Boscoreale and about the same, Augustan, date. On one of them is a scene of Priam kneeling to kiss the hand of Achilles, supplicating for the return of the body of the slain Hector, a representation that became popular as a relief on sarcophagi of a later period. The scene on the second cup is based on the legend of Philoctetes and may refer to a lost play of that name by Euripides (Philoctetes was bitten by a snake on his way to the Trojan War; he missed the first ten years and only arrived in time to kill Paris). Both cups had some of their details picked out with gilding and both had been signed, in stippled letters, by their maker. His name was Cheirisophos and on one cup it was in Greek lettering (the Priam and Achilles), and on the other in Latin, although still following the Greek form of his name – he probably came from Asia Minor. Both cups have the name Silius scratched on the base, presumably a former owner, and the Philoctetes cup also has added the total weight of the pair.

Also from the far north beyond the frontiers of the empire at Haagerup in Fynen comes a small late Roman silver bowl that is an interesting piece. It imitates in silver a form that is more acceptable as glasswork, more to be expected as a mold-blown glass bowl. It was probably made in Roman Gaul rather than the Mediterranean world.

The largest group of Roman silverware found beyond the frontiers was discovered in 1868 at Hildesheim near Hanover, Germany. It had been carefully buried in a pit roughly four by three feet and five feet deep. In all there were some 70 items, including some fragments, and it is thought to represent the household plate belonging to a Roman commander who was campaigning against the Germanic tribes. The hoard overall presents a slight problem in dating – most of the pieces seem to date from between 50 BC and AD 50, essentially falling within the Augustan period like so many of the

other northern finds. But, there is the name of Marcus Aurelius done in stippling on the base of one of the pieces and this therefore looks toward an early second century AD date for its deposit at least, when the name had become prominent. It would seem that most of the pieces were therefore family heirlooms. The hoard included six large dishes; eight trays; eight bowls; nine cups; two urns and a bucket; four *paterae*; a candelabrum and two folding tripod-tables upon which large dishes would be stood. A number of the pieces were also partly gilt.

Although the sheer bulk of the silver is overwhelming, two of the pieces in the hoard were of outstanding importance, possibly, even, the finest surviving examples of their type. One is a circular dish with two short side handles and a zone of elaborately engraved lotus and honeysuckle around the inner edge, framing the central, high relief *emblema*. This is a superb seated figure of the goddess Athena which stands proud, almost three dimensional, of the background. The goddess is clad in flowing drapery and wears a highly ornate helmet. Under her left arm she nurses her circular shield and rests her right hand on a tall 'walking' stick with what appears to be a snake's head. Her familiar, the owl, is perched on a heap of rocks in

front of her. The dish was gilded, except for the flesh parts of the goddess. The craftsmanship of the piece and the modelling point to its Hellenistic antecedents. It must have been a Greek artist who carried out this commission, probably somewhere in the eastern Empire. It has a number of affinities with the great Africa *emblema* dish from Boscoreale.

The other major *emblema* dish from the Hildesheim treasure has a similar well-engraved tendril motif surrounding the central *emblema* which here is the very realistically modelled head and shoulders of the infant Hercules. He is grasping a serpent in each hand, an allusion to the legend of how he throttled two snakes that crept into his cradle (it became a very popular

Left: Silver medallion cup with a seated Athena from the Hildesheim treasure. Romer Pelizaeus Museum, Hildesheim.

Below left: A silver-handled bucket or situla from the Chaourse treasure. British Museum, London.

Right: From Chattuzange a silver skillet with a highly ornamented handle is a very high class version of the more common soldier's mess tin. British Museum, London.

Below: Silver pepper pot in the form of a squatting negro boy from the Chaourse treasure is rather unusual and is closer in spirit to South Italian terracotta pieces of 500 years earlier. British Museum, London.

type on the reverse of many Greek coins, especially of Heraclea in southern Italy). The interesting point here is that the Hercules bust is repoussé work and was added to the dish. The Athena medallion was cast, and plaster molds for such pieces have been found at Mit Rahineh (Memphis) in Egypt. Two other *emblema* dishes among the treasure have modelled heads of Cybele and Attis, but they have plain, not ornamented, bowls and are of much lesser style.

After the numerous examples of fine Roman silver plate that survive from the first century there is very little by comparison from the second century and certainly no outstanding pieces like the *emblema* dishes. Of the groups that survive, most come from northern Gaul, having been buried in the troubles that wracked the 'Gallic Empire' with its series of usurper emperors in the third quarter of the century. A good example of a fine set of household silver buried at a time of danger about AD 270 comes from Chaourse, near Montcornet, Aisne, France. It was found in 1883 in a field and had been deposited wrapped in a cloth. Coins were also found with it, the latest being a piece of the usurper Gallic emperor Postumus of AD 267. The indications are that the hoard was buried shortly afterward, in the reign of Gallienus. The hoard is a fairly homogeneous group of domestic plate and includes some quite attractive items. There are plain silver drinking cups, jugs, deep situla-like bowls, shallow plates, hemispherical bowls, flanged and also fluted bowls, some mirrors, a strainer and a pepper pot. The flanged bowls have engraved ornament on them that includes animals such as a lion among the floral ornament. The two fluted bowls are particularly attractive, one with a six-leafed star pattern as the central motif. A small dish had a low-relief ornament, heavily gilded, in the center with a standing figure of Mercury holding his caduceus and flanked by two of his familiars, a ram and a cock. There are two unusual pieces in the hoard. One is a silver strainer which is hinged to fit into the attached funnel. Its punched holes make up floral and geometric patterns and the piece is unique. The other unusual piece was a pepper pot modelled as a squatting negro boy, the holes for the pepper being punched in the top of his head. This piece was not only functional but also highly decorative on the table.

Of the same period, the hoard from Chattuzange-le-Goubet, Drôme, produced a good example of the typical saucepan or skillet better known in bronze as a normal piece of army issue equipment (the ancient version of the modern soldier's canteen). This example has an attractive and satisfying shape and the handle is decorated in relief with a figure of Felicitas between two rosettes at the rounded top with, below her, a small rustic shrine and, below that, a woman who is offering a sacrifice at an altar. The side elements that serve to strengthen the handle have a pair of dogs lying down and baskets of fruits.

A number of large groups of silver plate survive from the fourth century. The largest hoard yet discovered was found at Kaiseraugst near Basle, Switzerland, in December 1961 and January 1962. It had been buried in a chest inside the late Roman fortress and consisted of 257 items, made up of 187 silver coins, medallions and ingots and a table service so luxurious that it was first thought to have belonged to the emperor Julian (AD 360–363) himself. Further work on the coins and the stamps on the silverware inclined more toward a date of AD 350/351 for its burial. Of particular note are two large dishes; one was circular with a central partly gilt and niello medallion with a view of a seaside city, the sea in front of it teeming with fish and with five fishing boats manned by cupids. The rim has eight panels, alternately geometric designs and hunting scenes. The other great dish is only slightly smaller and less grand than the great Oceanus dish from Mildenhall (see below). Known as the Achilles Dish, it is an eight-sided plate with scenes from the life of Achilles. The central medallion shows the discovery of Achilles among the daughters of Lycomedes by Odysseus and Diomedes (a subject already noted as being popular on sarcophagi reliefs). Two inscriptions on the base give the weight of the dish and that it was made by Pausylypos in Thessalonica. Such scenes from the life of Achilles, probably copied from superior tableware such as this, appear on the large fine red ware pottery *lanxes* (flat trays/dishes) made in Roman North Africa in the late fourth/early fifth century AD. Other items among the silver plate included two plain conical beakers; 22 spoons (including 14 of the rare swan's neck handle type); a fine candelabrum (rather like the one from the Beaurains/Arras treasure), and a deep oblong dish with wide flanges and a semicircular projection at its end. Engraved in the center of the base is a fish with a worm in its mouth; the motif may explain the unusual shape of the dish and hence its use for fish. A particularly attractive little item is a silver statuette of a nude Venus standing on a solid silver base. In her right hand she holds up a mirror while combing her long tresses (Venus Anadyomen, 'braiding her hair') with her left. A piece of specifically Christian silver was a small utensil (possibly for dividing up the Host) with a spoon at one end and a pointed spatula at the other, pierced with a chi-rho monogram. Although the treasure did not belong to a member of the imperial family, its owner was obviously a person of very high standing and he must have caused the treasure to be buried during one of the many crises in this area of Switzerland early in the second half of the third century.

A major treasure from the second half of the fourth century AD was found on the Esquiline Hill in Rome in 1793. It is of particular importance since there are few other objects that can be specifically attributed to fourth-century workshops in Rome. The best-known pieces are the Casket of Projecta and her domed toilet

Top: The great eight-sided Achilles dish from the Kaiseraugst treasure, Switzerland, shows episodes from his early life, culminating in his discovery among the daughters of Lycomedes in the central tondo.

Above: The charming and unusual little silver statuette of Venus braiding her hair has its inspiration in statues of Aphrodite carved in stone in the fourth century BC. Kaiseraugst treasure. Römermuseum, Augst.

Above right: Silver-gilt statuette of Alexandria, one of four personifications of the principal cities of the Empire which were probably fittings for a carrying chair. Esquiline treasure. British Museum, London.

Above: The Projecta Casket from the Esquiline treasure is an important piece that combines Christian and pagan elements. British Museum, London.

Bottom: A pair of flat silver dishes from the Carthage treasure. That on the left identifies the family associated with the treasure, the Cresconii; on the right, the inscription includes the Christian chi-rho monogram. British Museum, London.

Below: The silver covered bowl from the Carthage treasure could easily be mistaken for a piece by a modern silversmith. British Museum, London.

casket. The Projecta Casket is an oblong box with a high lid of truncated pyramid shape. It was a wedding gift to the lady Projecta and has a wreathed roundel in the center of the lid showing the husband and wife. The decoration in repoussé panels on the lid and within the arcaded panels on the body are scenes connected with the marriage rituals. An inscription on the edge of the lid, preceded by a chi-rho monogram, reads: SECUNDE ET PROIECTA VIVATIS IN CHRISTO ('Secundus and Projecta, may you live in Christ'). Projecta may be identified with the lady for whom Pope Damasus (AD 366–384) personally wrote an epitaph; it used to be in the Church of S Martino ai Monti, close to the spot where the treasure was found. Projecta's husband, Secundus, was probably L Turcius Secundus, the Turcii being a prominent Roman family of the period.

The other piece, Projecta's domed silver toilet casket, is actually represented being carried by a female servant on the back panel of her bridal casket. The toilet casket is a high-domed, cylindrical box with alternate decorated flat and plain fluted panels on the hinged lid and with figures of the Muses represented in the alternate concave and flat panels of the bottom part. Inside, the casket was fitted with a thin bronze plate, pierced to take the silver cosmetic containers. Any toilet silver, apart from mirrors, is rare at this period and these two pieces are outstanding items of late Roman silverware. Various other silver vessels formed part of the treasure, including square and circular dishes with a monogram in their centers that has been interpreted as 'Projecta Turcii' (one of the circular silver dishes, of a set of four, had an inscription scratched under the rim SCVT[ELLAE]IIII PV = 'the set of four weighed five Roman pounds'); a tall embossed flask; silver saucepans (skillets); six sets of highly ornamental horse trappings and four silver-gilt statuettes (probably fittings from a chair) that represented the *Tyches*, personifications, of the four principal cities of the Roman empire: Rome, Constantinople, Alexandria and Antioch. As it so often the case, the reason for concealing such an outstanding collection is not known. Certainly it cannot be later than the sack of Rome in AD 410 by the Visigothic king Alaric.

From the Hill of St Louis, Carthage, on the southern frontiers of the empire comes another great silver treasure that can be associated with a named family, the Cresconii. Inscribed in the center of a ribbed dish, around the tondo, is D D ICRESCONI CLARENT, thereby associating the group with a powerful Roman North African family who are well known from deeds and offices held in the second half of the fourth century AD. Other pieces present included some flanged bowls, one with chased scenes in low relief of shepherds and their charges around the rim and in the central medallion. A very unusual vessel is a covered silver bowl on a high tapering foot that is very modern in the pure simplicity of its lines.

Although items of silver plate have been found in virtually every province of the empire, it is rather strange that Britain seems to have had much more than its fair share of such discoveries, both in hoards and single pieces. During the excavations of the temple of Mithras in the Walbrook, London, in 1954, a small decorated, cylindrical box was found that held a strainer or infuser. When restored it could be seen that the series of lively scenes of conflict between men and animals around the outside seemed to relate to the mithraic mysteries. The object was probably used as an infuser, perhaps to prepare some kind of herbal drug for the initiates.

From the hoard of silverware found at Mildenhall, Suffolk, about 1942, comes not quite the largest but surely the most splendid Roman silver plate to survive – the so-called Oceanus dish. It dates from about AD 360, is almost two feet across and weighs over 18 pounds (8.256 kg). In the central tondo is a facing, bewhiskered head of the ocean god with four dolphins starting from his beard and wild hair. A circular frieze of fantastic marine animals and Nereids surrounds Oceanus and is in its turn surrounded by the great outer frieze that represents Bacchic revels. Bacchus himself presides over it all (standing upside down in relation to Oceanus' head) while ecstatic satyrs, Maenads and a bearded figure of Pan whirl and cavort to the music of Pan-pipes and flutes. To the left, a drunken Hercules is held from falling over by two youthful satyrs. The whole impression of the decoration is one of violent movement. Two smaller dishes en suite show Pan playing his pipes and a Maenad a double flute, while the other has a dancing satyr and Maenad who holds her thyrsus and tambourine.

Among the rest of the 34 silver items in the treasure are several flanged bowls (one quite close to the Carthage Treasure shepherd example); a covered bowl; a pair of stemmed goblets; a fluted and handled bowl; a series of ladles with dolphin handles and a number of spoons with inscriptions or monograms in their bowls. The spoons have a definite Christian connotation (PASCENTIA VIVAS, and PAPITTEDO VIVAS) which is further underlined by three spoons which have the chi-rho monogram flanked by alpha and omega. A similarly inscribed spoon, the survivor of four found near Biddulph, Stafford, is typical of a number known from the fourth century.

While the obviously Christian items in the Mildenhall Treasure were for secular use, the 27 silver (plus one gold) items found at Water Newton, near Peterborough, Cambridgeshire, in 1975, were just as obviously for religious use and are the earliest group of Christian silver yet known from the whole of the Roman Empire. There were nine vessels (some fragmentary) and nineteen plaques plus a circular gold disc. It was the inscriptions with their Christian chi-rho monograms and dedications that caused an archaeological sensation. Other items, including eight of the leaf-shaped

Above: A silver goblet from the Mildenhall Treasure. British Museum, London.

Above center: A silver ladle with dolphin handle from the Mildenhall treasure. British Museum, London.

Top: When found in the Wallbrook mithraeum the decorated silver pyxis with its internal infuser was almost crushed flat. Restoration revealed it as an unusual ritual object probably used in initiation ceremonies. Museum of London, London.

Above right: Silver leaf-shaped plaque with a gilded chi-rho monogram in relief, flanked by A and W. Water Newton treasure. British Museum, London.

Top right: Part of the large treasure of silver plate from Mildenhall, Suffolk. The largest item was the great Oceanus dish (illustrated) with two smaller dishes en suite with Bacchic motifs. Also found were a number of stemmed goblets, a small silver bowl with an elaborate vine scroll on its broad rim, and a spoon with a leaf pattern in its bowl. British Museum, London.

Below right: A silver spoon, one of four from Biddulph, Staffordshire, with an engraved chi-rho monogram flanked by A and W in the bowl. Probably made in the eastern Mediterranean. British Museum, London.

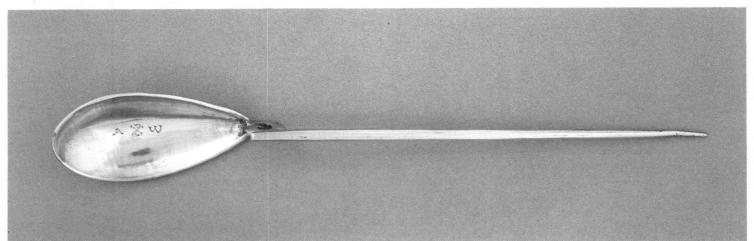

plaques and the circular gold disc, all bore the sacred symbol. A long-handled strainer also carried it, flanked by alpha and omega, at the end of its handle. A beautifully shaped, plain silver cup or goblet standing on a tall foot and with side handles (kantharos shape) is one of the simplest items of the treasure and it has even been suggested that it could have been used for the eucharist.

As surely pagan as the Water Newton Treasure was Christian is a large dish or lanx found in the river Tyne, near Corbridge (the Roman fort of *Corstopitum*), Northumberland, sometime during the eighteenth century. It is apparently the sole sad survivor of a larger hoard and almost certainly comes from a Mediterranean workshop. The design on it is completely classical and seems to relate to the series of deities worshipped on the island of Delos, especially Apollo and his twin sister Artemis. It is totally pagan in character but made 50 years after the empire became Christian under Constantine. The scene is an historical allusion to the sacrifice known to have been offered to Apollo on Delos by the emperor Julian the Apostate (who turned back to the pagan gods) in AD 363 as he moved east against the Persians. It must have reached Britain in the baggage of a very high ranking official and was, as usual, concealed at a time of trouble and never recovered.

A little later in its deposit, in the 380s or early 390s AD, is the most recently found hoard, the Thetford Treasure in 1979. A 'mixed bag' of 81 items, it consisted of a lot of jewellery, principally 22 gold finger rings, four pendants, five gold necklaces, three silver strainers and 33 silver spoons. The spoons are extremely interesting because of the sheer number present, let alone their inscriptions and decoration. They appear to have formed part of the temple plate of the god Faunus, a pastoral Roman deity rarely seen before in an archaeo-

logical context. The combination of the spoons and the jewellery, the gemstones and single gold buckle is very odd. A temple hoard and the apparent jeweller's stock-in-trade together do not produce a ready explanation. All save two of the spoons are inscribed and 12 of these refer to the Latian god Faunus. Two of the spoons are really outstanding: they have, respectively, parcel-gilt decoration with a triton and a panther. The former is of the curled duck-handle variety similar to pieces from the Kaiseraugst Treasure; it is inscribed DEINARI in the bowl under the triton. The panther spoon is the more normal long-handled type and also has an inscription, in niello, on the handle to the god: DEII-FAVNINARI. A third spoon with decoration in the bowl has a fish with a plant-like object before it. Like so many late Roman treasures this hoard was found by accident and only became known nearly a year after its recovery, by which time its major archaeological context had been lost.

One last piece of Roman plate is an object that is not only extremely well known but also, from time to time, highly controversial – the Antioch Chalice. It takes its name from having been found near Antioch in Syria in 1910. It is actually two items because there is an undecorated silver cup that sits within the highly ornate, pedestalled outer cup. Here we see two representations of Christ and 10 apostles, all set within a gilded openwork of scrolls and vines. It is probably the earliest known Christian chalice to survive (if the Water Newton cup is disregarded) and belongs to the late fourth or early fifth century AD, the period of the so-called Theodosian Revival. Many have argued that the inner cup is the one used at the Last Supper, but it is an argument that lacks support. Whichever way it is viewed, emotively or prosaically, it is still one of the most splendid silver objects of the late Roman world, bordering on the late antique.

Gold plate or large objects in the precious metal are very rare survivals from the Roman empire. Most of the gold that has been recovered tends to be in the form of jewellery or gold coins and medallions. A curious, almost enigmatic, piece in solid gold is the bust of the emperor Marcus Aurelius (AD 161–180). This remarkable piece was found at Avenches in Switzerland. Roman Avenches (Aventicum) was a fairly large, reasonably prosperous town with its amphitheater, temples and so on, but for this gold bust to appear there is very strange. The workmanship is good, the mood of the philosopher emperor is well caught but the reason for its provision in such a quantity of the precious metal is unknown. It stands as one of the finest, and largest, surviving pieces of gold sculpture from the Roman world.

To turn from the precious metals to the baser ones of bronze (and lower), much more survives, particularly in terms of small sculptures or votives. Bronze was never thrown away, if what it represented was out of fashion or broken it could always be remelted and reworked. It was not uncommon in antiquity for bronze and copper tools to be weighed on issue out to workmen and for them to be weighed again upon their return just to check that no metal had been removed

for the workman's profit. Most fine bronzes that survive have done so because they were rendered inaccessible by a disaster, as at Pompeii and Herculaneum; were buried for safekeeping and never retrieved, such as temple pieces; were placed in a grave with no intent of recovery and were spared the visitations of tomb robbers; or they were revered because of misinterpretation and thus not destroyed, like the Marcus Aurelius statue on the Capitol at Rome.

It is an anachronism that the two best-known surviving sculptural bronzes that most people think about or envisage when Roman bronzes are mentioned are not, in fact, Roman. Despite this, they are so interlinked with the early legends and iconography of Rome that they cannot be omitted. These two bronzes are the Wolf and Twins and the head of Brutus, both in the Capitoline Museum, Rome. The Capitoline Wolf is one of the most potent symbols of Rome but stylistically the piece is Etruscan work with Ionic Greek overtones and probably dates from the end of the sixth or early fifth centuries BC. It was a well-known bronze in ancient Rome; Cicero probably refers to this actual piece in his Catiline orations when he mentions a wolf and twins on the Capitoline Hill that was struck by lightning, destroying one of the suckling twins. The she-wolf was

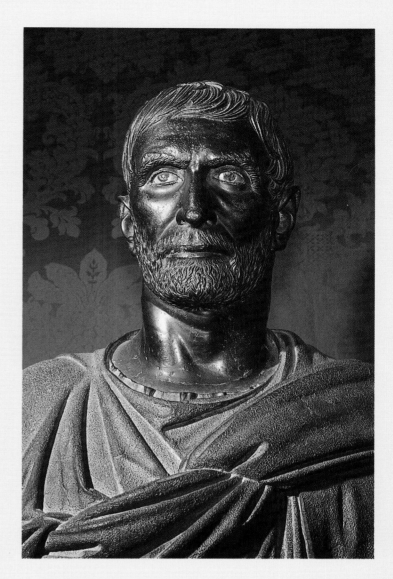

moved about in late antiquity and early medieval times; for long it stood in front of the Lateran. The twins now present were added in a restoration paid for by Pope Sixtus IV (1471–1484) and carried out by a Tuscan sculptor, Antonio Pollaiolo (1429–1498).

The other major piece, the head of Brutus (said by some to be L Junius Brutus, the founder of the Republic) is also a subject of contention as to its date, let alone who it purports to represent. Some consider it a work of the late Republic, others, more probably correct, assign it to the late fourth century BC from an Etruscan workshop. It certainly has many resemblances in style and technique with other known pieces from the period. The intensity of the gaze, which catches everyone's attention, is because the eyes were worked separately and then inserted into the head. The head was presented to the City of Rome by Cardinal Ridolfo Pio da Carpi in 1564.

Whatever the date, these two almost certainly Etruscan pieces are the epitome of Rome in bronzework and there can be no disputing that each is a powerful masterpiece. The Romans learned a lot about metalworking techniques from the Etruscans and then proceeded to improve upon what they had learned. The casting of small bronzes did not present many problems

since they could often be cast solid in a basic two-part mold if they were simple enough in their design. To cast larger pieces needed great expertise and control over the molten metal at all times to produce an even flow. The danger was that the metal would bubble and trap air as it was poured into the mold. Larger pieces were often cast in several different molds in sections and then the whole joined together. Casting faults that did occur in the larger pieces could often be cosmetically patched, but often time has been unkind and the pieces have dropped off (as with the bronze head of Hadrian from the Thames). Lost-wax casting (*cire perdue*) could be used for making fine, one-off pieces with detailed decoration. An original model (probably in clay) would be built up and the 'final' version modelled on to it in wax. This wax model was then invested with fine clay, leaving some vent holes at strategic places that could later be concealed by reworking. The whole was then fired in a kiln or oven. The wax melted and ran off, leaving a gap between the model and the skin. Careful pouring in of molten metal would produce a bronze casting within the clay structure. The clay had to be broken to release the piece, which was then finished by hand. Often the original core was left within the casting.

Above: The superbly studied 'Boxer,' created by Apollonius of Athens. Museo Nazionale, Rome.

Below: Bronze appliqué of a garlanded Lictor carrying his emblems of office, the *fasces* and axe. British Museum, London.

Center left: Head of a young man in bronze from Capella di Picenardi, Parma, that has all the characteristics of a formal late Republican period portrait bust. Louvre, Paris.

Below: A striking, authoritative pose and gesture in the lifesize bronze statue of the consul Aulus Metels of the first century BC. Museo Archeologico, Florence.

Left: Bronze portrait head from a statue of Augustus made all the more lifelike by the inset eyes. From Meroe, Sudan. British Museum, London.

The Romans mastered the use of bronze portrait sculpture quite early in the Republic and some very striking pieces were produced. They share with the stone sculpture the same austere 'presence' that sees its origins in the family funerary portraits. Basic characteristics, such as the 'Roman' nose can be noted quite early. By contrast there are a number of pieces that are of the late Republic but are more Hellenistic in character if not in actual manufacture – good examples of these are the Boxer by Apollonius of Athens at the end of the first century BC, now in the Museo Nazionale, Rome, and the 'Spinario,' a lad removing a thorn from his left foot, which may be a first century BC copy of a Hellenistic piece. Both are, nevertheless, popular masterpieces of the bronzeworker's craft.

The 'presence' that a Roman bronzeworker could produce in a late Republic statue is well demonstrated in the togate figure identified as the consul Aulus Metels. His stance, with right arm uplifted, is very reminiscent of the later 'ad locutio' of the emperor addressing his troops, and he makes an interesting comparison with the stone sculpture of the senator holding his ancestral busts. A bronze appliqué of the Augustan period shows us a Lictor who would have accompanied such dignitaries, carrying the symbolic bundle of *fasces* (rods) with the axe blade standing clear of them, and wearing a garland. Both bronzes, Metals and the Lictor, are superbly detailed and they evidence the bronze caster's craft; Metels is virtually lifesize, the Lictor only $7\frac{1}{4}$ inches (18.5 cm).

Imperial portraits, be they in stone or bronze, were of obvious importance in the empire. They had to be shipped to all parts as a record of the wearer of the purple, if nothing else. Often such busts would have to serve as models for the production of dies for coin portraits in those cities empowered to produce their own money. Stone sculpture was easier to provide but bronze portraits could be for specific use in temples and the like. A most striking (even disturbing because of the eyes) portrait of Augustus had a very chequered history. Excavated at Meroe in the Sudan, far beyond the Roman boundaries of empire, it seems to have been carried off as booty, broken perhaps from a portrait cult statue in the temple at Aswan on the southern boundaries of Egypt when it was captured by the legendary Queen Candace in 24 BC. Punitive expeditions followed her retreat south but the emperor's portrait was never recovered. The effect of the eyes was obtained by making their whites from marble and insetting the irises with glass in a ring of copper. This was almost certainly a deliberately achieved effect because Suetonius records that Augustus thought there was divine power in his eyes and 'he was delighted if anyone at whom he looked sharply let his face fall, as before the radiance of the sun.' Pliny merely remarked that Augustus had 'eyes like horses.' Both are right in their own way, looking at this remarkable, but probably mass-produced for colonial use, bronze.

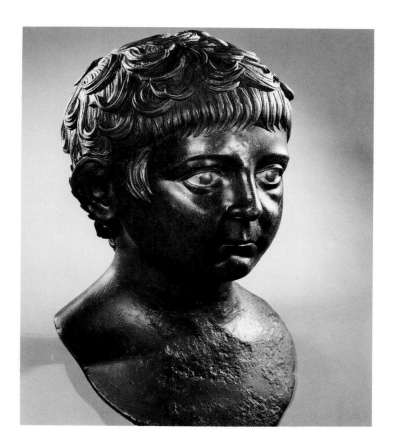

A similar overlifesize bronze head of a young member of the Imperial family is difficult to identify, but is of the highest quality. It dates to the first century AD and the downward gaze from the hollow, once inlaid, eyes contrasts sharply with the Augustus bronze. There is a tendency towards an 'Alexander' look about the head, particularly enhanced by the style of the hair, which in itself might point more to the Augustan era than later.

A charming study of a child in New York that is possibly the very young Nero serves to remind us how people can change in their facial features as well as character. This delightful study in bronze is perhaps a little difficult to equate with the full, fleshy faced portraits of Nero just before his suicide in AD 68 at the age of 31. A more athletic figure is presented in the military figure of Nero from Barking Hall, Suffolk, with its fine detail and enamel. The upward gaze and heroic stance all hark back to god-like classical antecedents.

Two bronze heads of emperors connected with Britain survived because of their destruction in antiquity. The bronze head of Claudius, recovered from the river Alde in Suffolk, was probably looted from his temple at Colchester at the Boudiccan sack of the city in AD 60 (much the same fate as had occurred with the bronze Augustus from Meroe). It is quite a good study of the emperor, made very human by its large ears. Similarly, the bronze head of Hadrian from the Thames must have been wrenched from an official statue, probably standing in the basilica, in the troubles at the end of the third century. It had proved a little difficult in the casting and patches had been discreetly applied in

Right: Alexandrian bronze statuette of a youth in fetters with a pair of fish hung around his neck. Probably a steelyard weight. Private collection.

Above: A small study in bronze of a crouched sick old lady holding a cup, found at Vichy, France. Louvre, Paris.

several places where the metal was not particularly good. These have fallen off over the centuries and therefore give an insight into the bronzeworkers' art. On the Capitol in Rome the equestrian statue of Marcus Aurelius with right hand outstretched in a typical 'ad locutio' gesture of addressing his troops has only recently (1984) been moved inside the museum from its central position in the Piazza del Campidoglio. It had been there since 1538 when it had been brought from the Lateran. It is among the finest statues of its type surviving, even still retaining some of its gilding, and it owes its survival to the mistaken medieval belief that it represented Constantine the Great, the first Christian emperor. Numerous other Imperial portraits are known in bronze from various parts of the empire, but predominantly from the eastern sectors. As the years went by they all began to lose the characteristic look of the earlier centuries AD. By the late third and fourth centuries many of those statues which have come down to us share a very bland look about their features that already looks forward to the empty-faced vacuous portraits of the late antique.

As with objects made in various materials, it is invariably in the smaller items that one finds aspects to delight the eye or to amuse. Many of the larger pieces that survive, of unidentified individuals, are only of interest because of their very survival. A number of the pieces from the Bay of Naples sites fall into this category and, had they not been engulfed, would certainly have found their way into the melting pot long since. Among the small bronzes it is possible to find very attractive pieces that may not be great works of art but they do, by virtue of the element of himself that the craftsman has managed to put into them, speak to us over the centuries. Similarly, they can make the past more immediate and often give an insight into the social and economic conditions of the period. Pre-eminent in this respect are the bronze-casters of Alexandria in Egypt. Their work is very immediate, it may give rise to amusement in viewing the piece, or to pathos. Two examples will suffice to bring this out. A characteristic product of the Alexandrian workshops are small studies of what nowadays would be called the socially deprived or the butts of society. Dwarfs seem to be of particular interest and we find very amusing studies, a dwarf dancing girl oblivious to all as she

pirouettes, emulating a ballerina as best she may on her stubby legs; or the male dwarf, naked except for his chlamys over his shoulder, who balances a fairly large *lekythos* (in relation to his stature) on his shoulder while he makes haste to relieve himself. Such small studies could only have been made for amusement (he is $3\frac{1}{4}$ inches (8.3 cm) high)) since they have no functional purpose. Yet even functional items can have far more to them than might be thought warranted. Objects such as steelyard weights, which only served to be hung from the arm of the scales to adjust the balance, can be excessively ornamented in relation to their mundane function. Echoes of punishment meted out in the Middle Ages to erring tradesmen seem to be present in a small bronze weight that shows a nude youth, his upraised hands secured in a wooden clamp or handcuffs (just as prisoners are shown in ancient Egyptian reliefs). Around his neck dangle two fish. Was he a fisherman who gave short weight one wonders, especially as the loop on the crown of his head shows

Left: Alexandrian bronze of a grotesque dwarf balancing a wine jar on his shoulder and about to relieve himself. Private collection.

Above: A delightful study in a small Alexandrian bronze of the first century BC/AD of a young girl dwarf pirouetting and playing castanets. British Museum, London.

that he was himself actually a weight.

Pathos comes clearly to the fore in a similarly small-sized bronze (4 inches high) of a crouched old lady holding a cup, found at Vichy, France. The same subject has also appeared in larger stone sculpture (Capitoline Museum, Rome) but somehow the small bronze is not only arresting, it is very much more alive. There is an element best described by the French as *sympathetique* here and it is something that is also present in many instances in bronze representations of animals. The leaping pig, his back legs on the stand and his front trotters flying forward, from Herculaneum is a case in point. He may not be to everyone's taste nowadays but he was appreciated by someone as a suitable household ornament.

Fine casting of thin bronze with abundant detail can be found on prosaic objects that have been embellished so as to raise them up into a very different category. Furniture can be enhanced to almost any high degree and Roman couches lent themselves particularly to the addition of appliqués or modelled additions. A particularly pleasing and lifelike study of the head of a wild ass turned sharply back immediately captures the animal's spirit. It served as a fulcrum finial on the headboard of a couch; obviously one from a very wealthy household. In much the same vein, that is ornamentation with fine work of a prosaic object, is a bronze Silenus mask that served as one of a pair of handles for a wine bucket. The wild companion of Dionysus was a worthy and appropriate decoration for a container that held the god's gift to mankind. Splendid examples of the very highest quality as the piece illustrated are excessively rare (there are less than a dozen known). Copper, silver and iron inlay were all used to enhance the features of the piece, the fillet across the Silenus' brow and the wreath of ivy and berries that he wears. He appears on wine bucket handles in profusion, coming right down to just a schematic satyr head placed on a vine leaf, and is a popular motif right across the empire.

Left: Bronze mask of Silenus. This magnificent object was one of a pair as it formed part of the handle attachment of a situla, or wine bucket of the early first century AD. Private collection.

Below: Realistically modelled head of a wild ass in bronze inlaid with silver. Late first century AD. Originally part of the fittings of a couch. Private collection.

Above: Silvered bronze face mask and vizored parade helmet from Vize, Thrace. The face has been made quite lifelike and the wearer would look out through the pupils pierced in the eyes of the bronze face. Arkeoloji Müzelerini, Istanbul.

Left: The tombstone of Marcus Caelius, a centurion of the Eighteenth Legion, shows his armor and its decorations of *phalerae*, gold torques and thick bracelets as well as the fact that he has been awarded the *corona civica* (civic crown of oak leaves) for having saved a citizen's life with danger to himself. Rheinisches Landesmuseum, Bonn.

Above: Tombstone of Gnaius Museus, *aquilifer* (standard bearer) of the Fourteenth Legion, detailing his armor and the eagle-headed standard that he carried. Magonza Museum.

Above right: Bronze parade helmet with a face mask from Ribchester. The helmet is decorated with fighting figures in relief. Such helmets were only issued to crack cavalry regiments. British Museum, London.

Another area of bronzeworking that lent itself to ostentatious display was military equipment. The changing patterns of arms and armor from the Republic to the late empire are best documented from the tombstones of the army. We can see all ranks and levels of officer as they had been seen in life, proudly displaying their insignia and *phalerae* (awards). The latter, like campaign medals or gallantry awards, are often illustrated in some detail on the stele. A good example is the tombstone of Marcus Caelius, a centurion who perished in the great disaster in the German forests when three legions under P Quinctilius Varus were ambushed and wiped out in 9 BC in the reign of Augustus. Caelius' monument is a fine piece of sculpture that clearly shows his armor, *phalerae* and gold

torques as well as his symbol of office, the vine stick.

Not a lot of military equipment survives but helmets that were only for ceremonial purposes are magnificent items. They were issued only to crack cavalry regiments and to have seen a squadron in full ceremonial dress wearing decorated helmets such as that from Ribchester with its modelled high relief, or the silvered bronze facemask visor helmet from Vize, Thrace, must have been spectacular. Gladiators' helmets were also often highly embellished, along with the rest of their equipment, while their more normal issue was built for strength with no catching pieces to assist an opponent.

One last aspect of metalworking that ranges across the whole spectrum from utilitarian objects to miniature works of art is the coinage of Rome. Silver was at a

149

Above : A very fine example of a bronze gladiator's helmet with pierced vizor and griffon fronted crest. Found at Herculaneum, it was given by the Queen of Naples to Josephine. Louvre, Paris.

Top and center right : Cast bronze bar *circa* 274 BC with an elephant on one side and a sow on the other. The types may be a reference to the battle of Bene-

ventum and would make this piece the earliest Roman 'coin' with a historical reference on it. British Museum, London.

Right and bottom right : Orichalclum sestertius of Nero with a particularly fine portrait and a detailed representation on the reverse of a triumphal arch erected to commemorate the war against Parthia. Münzkabinett, Staatliche Museen, Berlin.

premium in the early days of the Republic and so the earliest coins of Rome were large cast pieces of bronze that went by weight. They had various devices or types on them that often alluded to Rome in their symbolism. One of the most interesting, cast about 274 BC, has an elephant on one side and a sow on the other. This is a direct allusion to the conflict between Pyrrhus of Epirus and Rome, when Rome was endeavoring to extend its rule over the Greek colonial cities of South Italy. At the battle of Beneventum in 275 BC the Indian elephants being used by Pyrrhus against the Roman army were frightened and stampeded into their own ranks by the Roman ruse of releasing pigs among them, and Rome won the day. Silver coinage was introduced soon afterward and the large, heavy and clumsy pieces of bronze were abandoned.

Bronze was not abandoned altogether for the coinage since it was the obvious base metal to use. There were various denominations, the aureus in gold, the denarius in silver, the sestertius in orichalcum (brass), the dupondius in bronze, the as in copper and then smaller pieces also in bronze. The comparatively large size of the sestertius lent itself to very fine portraits and interesting reverse types because finer detail could be achieved on the larger surface of the die from which the

coins were struck. There are particularly fine examples of sestertii struck under Nero and through into the first half of the second century AD. Often we find detailed representations of buildings or monuments for which the coins serve as the only contemporary record, or of ceremonies and allusions to the gods of Rome. Even larger pieces may have been used as specific gifts from the emperor and these occur in gold as well as base metals. A unique medallion of Marcus Aurelius presents a fine portrait of the emperor and a very interesting reverse type that shows Neptune, foot on a ship's prow, before the gate in a city wall. It may well be a reference to the god's involvement at the start of the Trojan War; shown here on the medallion are the walls of Troy that were breached by cunning and the Trojan Horse.

Commemorative pieces for special events are found that are multiple pieces of the ordinary coins. Often medallions in gold occur that are 5- or 10-aurei pieces. A splendid example found in Egypt at Aboukir has a pair of very fine portraits facing each other of the joint emperors Diocletian and Maximian, each dressed in rich consular robes and holding their eagle-tipped staff of office as consuls. The reverse represents the two emperors in the great consular procession of AD 287. They travel in a chariot drawn by four elephants and acknowledge the crowds from their lofty perch while the goddess of Victory flies above them to crown them both. Once again the combination of size and precious metal has produced a spectacular piece that is a miniature work of art and certainly a treasure. Another important historical event, probably a turning point for the whole Western world, is commemorated on a large gold medallion, a 9-solidus piece, of Constantine I, the Great. On the obverse he is shown associated with the sun god Sol and the god appears a second time there as the device on Constantine's shield in a four-horse chariot. Sol and Christ were often identified together in the early Christian world, as we see him in a mosaic under the Vatican in the tomb of the Julii. The reverse shows Constantine on horseback, preceded by a winged Victory holding a wreath and followed by a soldier carrying the legionary standard. This is a direct reference to Constantine's triumphal entry into Rome after defeating Maxentius at the battle of the Milvian Bridge, to the north of Rome, in AD 312. There he had received the vision or dream that was to turn the empire officially to the Christian faith and thus affect the subsequent history of Rome and the Western world.

Metal of any sort was hard won from the earth in antiquity. It all had value and it had the great advantage that it could be easily melted down and reused many times. Considering these factors it is quite amazing how much has survived in all metals. When some of the masterpieces are considered it is salutary to remember that if these survived the ages, how much more has either been lost or is still awaiting discovery.

Gold bracelet set with sapphires, emeralds and pearls, *circa* 3rd century AD. British Museum.

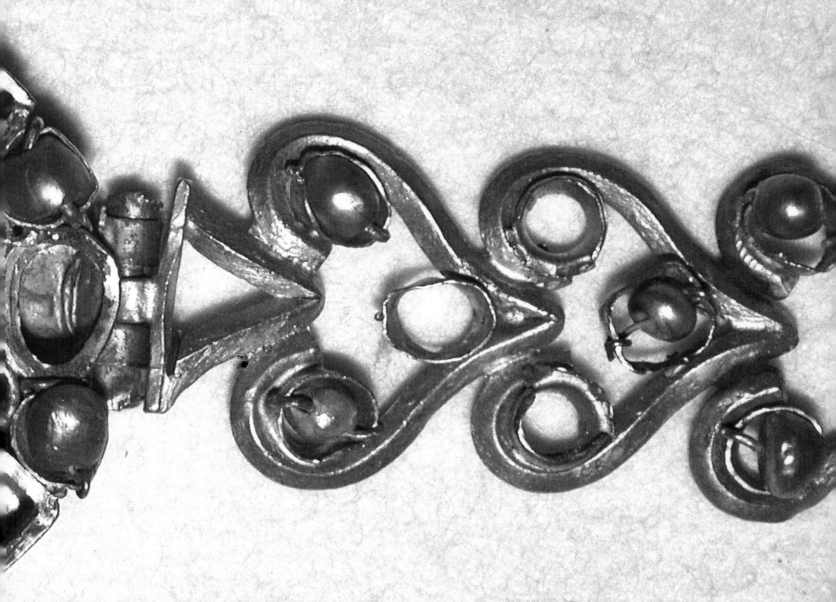

8.Jewelry

For most people the idea of ancient jewellery is centered on Egypt, Greece and perhaps Etruria. The wealth of gold jewellery that survived the depredations of the tomb robbers in Egypt is nothing short of miraculous when it is considered what a thriving trade tomb robbery was in Egypt for over 3000 years. However, much of the surviving jewellery from that period is funerary, made especially for burial with the dead. Greek and Hellenistic jewellery survives in quite large quantities, essentially again coming from tomb deposits. Likewise, the large quantities of Etruscan jewellery have invariably been found bedecked on skeletons. Roman jewellery is nowhere near as prolific in its survival as from any of the last named civilizations and, where it does survive, rarely is it as spectacular. There are a number of reasons for this. In the early days of the Republic there was little enough of the precious metal about for personal adornment. The Villanovan culture of northern Italy that preceded Rome relied largely on ornaments of bronze. The jewellery worn by Roman ladies in the last couple of centuries BC was almost certainly Etruscan, or made by Etruscan craftsmen and not readily distinguishable as a Roman product.

The other major factor affecting the provision of Roman jewellery, and thereby its survival, was the official attitude of the law and the disapproval that it expressed at ostentatious display. In the fifth century BC the Law of the Twelve Tables laid down guidelines and instructions relating to all manner of things, especially concerning conduct, and they also limited the quantity of gold allowed to be buried with the dead. A later law in the third century BC specified that a Roman lady was not allowed to wear jewellery amounting to more than half an ounce in weight. Some of the beautiful early chaplets, copying flower forms, were made of very light beaten gold, but they tended to be for funerary use rather than in life. The emphasis was upon gold in the laws was because it was such an overt sign of wealth and because silver was still not all that common in the Roman world. It was the Greek world of Athens and Macedon that controlled the major sources of silver. Another factor that should not be forgotten is that gold is virtually indestructible and will always maintain its good looks whereas silver does not survive so well. Silver is subject to the conditions of the ground in which it might have been buried and oxidizes easily in certain circumstances. Hence the survival rate of silver jewellery is far lower than that of gold and its apparent lack should not be misconstrued in relation to the gold.

There is a distinct difference between jewellery styles of the western and the eastern ends of the empire. The eastern is very much governed by its antecedents, the splendid pieces of Greece perhaps best seen in the recent discoveries in the royal Macedonian tomb at Vergina of the fourth century BC. Here, especially in the tomb of Phillip II, the father of Alexander the Great, was found gold jewellery and workmanship of the highest caliber, the wreaths and the solid gold box with its sunburst emblem on the lid taking their place among the finest surviving items of the period. Such magnificence was copied, as it is today, at different levels in society and at an economic level that was feasible. The Greek forms merged into the Hellenistic with no great changes. Craftsmanship is of a high order and while some of the pieces might appear too flamboyant to the modern eye it must be remembered that the basic material was relatively cheap and also that jewellery especially has to be ostentatious in warm countries otherwise in sunlight it means nothing (the same situation is found nowadays in eastern countries with ornate silver jewellery and brightly colored textiles). In the west jewellery tends to be more utilitarian, for example, the numerous brooches (fibulae) of 'safety pin' form that survive in bronze, silver and occasionally gold. Necklaces are not so ostentatious; there is a greater preference for thin chains, perhaps strung with semiprecious stones such as raw emeralds, topaz, aquamarines and the like.

The great centers for jewellery manufacture in the Roman world, outside Rome itself (where there is inscriptional evidence of goldsmiths' guilds), were at Antioch and Alexandria. In Egypt, gold was still available from local sources, as it had been in pharaonic times. Much gold came from the south, Nubia, in the form of gold dust as is seen represented in the wall paintings in the tomb chapels of the nobles of the New Kingdom (sixteenth–eleventh centuries BC). The other source was the mines in the Red Sea Mountains, especially the area of the Wadi Hammamat that ran from near Luxor (ancient Thebes) to the Red Sea. The old workings can still be seen, and for a slave or criminal to be sentenced to work there was tantamount to enduring a living death, with death as a welcome release. A great variety of semiprecious stones were also obtained from this area and many of them were utilized in an uncut or raw state, either being simply pierced for use on necklaces or earrings, or to be set as 'chunks' into vessels.

The evidence from the jewellery itself is very uneven, due to the circumstances of survival and retrieval. There is a certain amount of literary evidence, notably on materials and techniques in the writings of Pliny the Elder and the citations in the laws. Otherwise we must rely on the visual evidence of representations which, by their very nature of commemoration, tend to be funerary. Once again, most of this comes from the eastern end of the empire, from Egypt and Syria. In Egypt, continuing the ancient tradition of embalming, there are the mummy panel portraits, while in Syria for about a century and a half from AD 100 there are the carved stone funerary stele of Palmyra. Here the deceased, both male and female, are often represented heavily bedecked with jewellery of all sorts. But these

are more focused on oriental, Hellenistic styles and although within the period of the Roman empire (and Palmyra the trading caravan city was subservient to Rome), the jewellery is not properly speaking Roman.

A very large proportion of the gold jewellery surviving comes from Egypt where the old customs of providing for the dead did not really die out until after the official adoption of Christianity. The ancient practice of embalming was continued, first for the Greek colonists and then with the waves of Roman agricultural and bureaucratic families. An innovation was the painting of a portrait of the person during their

Above left: A very elaborate gold hair ornament from third-century Tunisia still with several of its sapphires, emeralds and pearls in place. British Museum, London.

Above: Mummy portrait painted in wax encaustic on board of a young man, 'Ammonius,' from Antinoe, Egypt. He wears heavy gold rings on his fingers and clasps a gold embossed chalice. Louvre, Paris.

lifetime on a board in wax encaustic. They are the first easel portrait paintings in history. These were kept in the house during life and then inserted as a panel painting set in the mummy wrappings over the face of the deceased when the time came. From this source, especially from the Roman cemeteries excavated at

Hawara in the Fayuum in Egypt by Sir Flinders Petrie, we have a remarkable portrait gallery of the upper-middle-class settlers of the first to third centuries AD. In many instances their direct gaze still has a rather disturbing quality about it. Jewellery was not restricted to women, men wore rings and also diadems. A portrait panel of a young man known as 'Ammonius' found at Antinoe shows a very thoughtful fellow who wears heavy gold rings on his left hand holding a wreath of flowers and, a little unusually with such panels, he holds a gem-encrusted, footed gold chalice in his right hand. The gold rings with their self flat bezels (as against having intaglios mounted on the bezel) are more in keeping with earlier Egyptian forms of heavy signet rings. Presumably the chalice is set with large, possibly uncut, semiprecious stones, or it may be silver gilt with glass simulating more valuable stones.

The portrait panels of the women that illustrate jewellery are far more numerous, as may be expected. Naturally they wanted to be painted wearing their best or favorite pieces and hence they provide us with a useful framework for dating certain styles of jewellery.

It must always be borne in mind, however, that although the panel portrait might be fairly closely dated, the portrait from life could also show the lady wearing family heirloom jewellery that was much earlier. There is a great variety in the styles of the popular drop earrings, some of which appear to have been quite heavy. A portrait in Vienna shows a young woman with bar earrings, each with a triple drop with, apparently, pearls on the end. This is a new type that was introduced from Western Asia in the mid-first century AD. Her two necklaces are of typical forms that have survived. The lower one is a heavily ribbed piece in gold with a central medallion which has either a facing Medusa head or a lion's mask. Her upper, second, necklace is of a commoner type made up of gold barrel beads interspersed with a green bead that could be emerald from the Red Sea Mountains of Egypt. Similar green beads occur in western European finds, a fairly similar necklace appearing in the Beaurains/Arras hoard.

Choker-type necklaces were popular, with a longer chain on a second necklace that could hang lower down.

This latter would normally have some kind of center-piece such as a medallion, a large stone in a gold setting, a gold crescent or perhaps a *bulla*. This was a large spherical, hollow piece worn as an amulet which was a very popular Etruscan piece, especially as a protective amulet worn by children. The solid nature of some of the necklaces represented in the mummy portraits and actual examples found indicate that comfort was not necessarily the first criteria in the design of a piece of jewellery. The sheer weight of some of these necklaces must have made them very uncomfortable to wear for any length of time. Amuletic properties were also associated with two other popular decorations; the wheel, which had magical connotations in both the east and west, with its overtones of eternity; and the crescent, which was generally hung upside down from a central point on its curved back. This is not of Roman origin but goes back to much earlier traditions, especially among the early desert nomads who revered the moon at night more than the destructive daytime sun. In the second century AD, a new form of decoration became popular on necklaces. This was the use of gold coins as pendants (and also on rings, much as gold sovereigns are used nowadays). The coin was generally a gold aureus that weighed just over 7 grams in the early Empire but was gradually reduced to 5 grams or

even less at times. Several such gold coin necklaces have been found in Egypt (interestingly because the gold aureus of the normal Roman world did not circulate there as a coin because Egypt still had its own currency based on Greek denominations). An example in the Metropolitan Museum, New York, has a series of aureii of Severus Alexander (AD 222–235) and another in Kansas City has 12 pieces ranging from the emperor Hadrian (AD 117–138) to Gordian III (AD 238–244). Eight such pieces, similarly mounted each in a filigree mount, were found with the great hoard of gold coins and medallions at Beaurains/Arras, France, in 1922. These spanned from Hadrian to Postumus (AD 259–268). They must have represented quite a large amount of wealth even without their gold settings. In the Late Antique and Byzantine period more ornate necklaces of this style became very popular, incorporating large medallions that added considerably to their weight. They also occur on marriage belts such as the late sixth-century examples from the Lambousa Treasure, Cyprus.

Once again the principal source of jewellery for the first century AD lies in the cities overwhelmed by Vesuvius. Some of the pieces were found in association with groups better known for their silver treasures. Among the jewellery at Boscoreale was a loop-in-loop chain with wheel terminals and two gold snake brace-

items that people fleeing in terror would seize. Hence perhaps not as much jewellery as one might expect to find in such prosperous cities has been recovered, except from the bodies of those who failed to escape.

There is a distinct contrast between gold bracelets produced in the central area of the empire and the eastern sectors. The western ones were usually quite simple and relatively light in weight, the eastern ones were much larger and heavier with a tendency to solid rather than hollow cast work. There is a liking for decorated terminals, the ever-popular snake heads (although they seem to go out of favor at the end of the first century AD in the west) and other cast motifs of gods and goddesses. Another typical product of the Alexandrian jeweller was a heavy ribbed bracelet that usually holds a heavy bezel into which a coin, intaglio or colored stone could sit. A pair of rather lighter, open-work bracelets feature the head of the Graeco-Roman god of the underworld, Serapis. The style is more Greek than Roman and can find its antecedents in the Hellenistic breast and hair ornaments with figures in quite high relief rising from similar plaques. These are known from northern Greece in the second century BC.

Above left: Gold chain necklace found at Memphis, Egypt, with five aureii of Lucius Verus, Julia Domna, and Severus Alexander (3), set in differing ornamental mounts separated by tubular gold spacers. Metropolitan Museum of Art, New York.

Above and right: Two gold snake bracelets (right) and a loop-in-loop gold chain (above) with wheel-shaped terminals found with the silver treasure from Boscoreale. Louvre, Paris.

lets. Snakes were a popular motif on bracelets, armlets and rings. Often the reptile's scales are indicated by incised lines or cross-hatching and the eyes made life-like by being set with a green or red colored stone. Although an obvious choice to be represented on a sinuous piece of jewellery, the snake was a sacred guardian of the hearth and was considered to have rejuvenative properties, so it could have been worn as a protective amulet. Simple bands of solid gold, some-times set with a single semiprecious stone, were also found. In the chest discovered in the House of Menan-der at Pompeii, which held the carefully wrapped silver tableware, there was also the jewellery of the lady of the house, giving a good idea of the various necklaces, bracelets, rings and so on, that a well-to-do Roman matron might own. In the disaster of AD 79 small portable valuables such as jewellery would be the first

A piece of jewellery that began as a utilitarian object among the Celts and was then adopted by the Romans in the west was the *fibula* (brooch). In effect it is an early form of safety pin. While literally thousands in bronze turn up on sites in the western empire, it is very rarely found in the east. This is largely due to climatic differences that affect dress and the accessories needed for it. Everyone, male and female, had to have their *fibulae* and it was only a matter of time before special pieces became available in the precious metals. Some, considering the utilitarian nature of the object, achieve high levels of craftsmanship and it is suspected that many of the really large, later third- and fourth-century crossbow *fibulae* were presentation pieces to senior ranking officers or civil servants. Several examples are known with names engraved on the bow and they are obviously not manufacturers' names (such as the well-

159

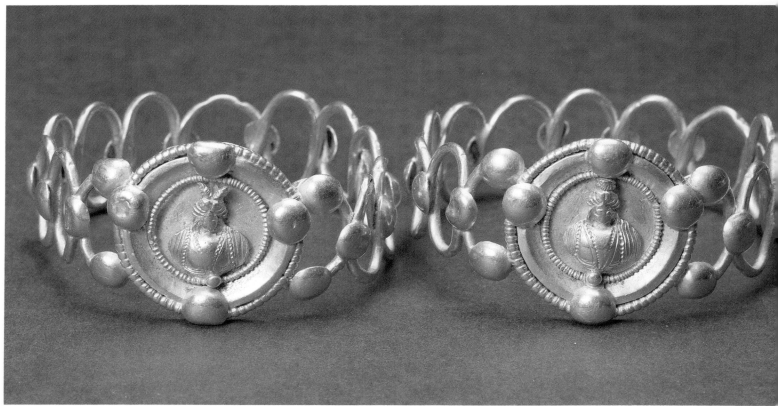

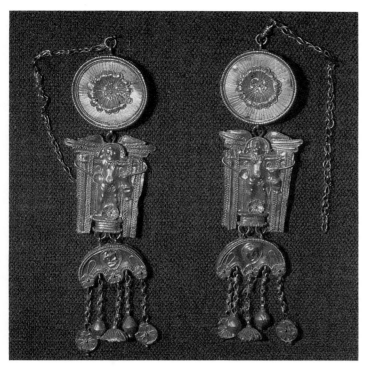

known Aucissa of the first century). A particularly splendid gold example was found at the Moray Firth, Scotland. The basic form has been substantially embellished by cusped motifs along the edges of the foot, hatched and plain triangles along the sides, crest (bow) at foot, and heavy ribbed decoration on the arms. This type of brooch features heavy decorative end knobs to the arms and one of the heavy terminals here unscrews to release the pin, quite a remarkable piece of work. Such brooches are invariably illustrated upside down in books (with their 'cross bow' head uppermost) but they were actually worn with the head downward; various contemporary illustrations demonstrate this. Sometimes they are worn in pairs, one on each shoulder, or just a single large specimen holds the folds of the material of the garment on the right shoulder, as can be seen on the ivory plaque showing the standing figure of the Vandal general Stilicho.

The commonest surviving item of Roman jewellery (after *fibulae*) are finger rings. Like other jewellery in early Rome, they were subject to strict regulations as to who might wear them and of what metal they should be. Pliny has a number of interesting comments about rings and their use. He begins by saying, 'The worst crime against mankind was committed by him who was the first to put a ring upon his fingers.' In early Rome only iron rings were worn and then 'solely as an indication of warlike prowess.' He notes that it was the Greeks who introduced the wearing of rings, but signet rings occur much earlier in ancient Egypt. At first only those who had been presented with a ring at public expense, such as ambassadors, wore them in order to equate them with distinguished foreigners with whom

Left: Alexandrian gold bracelets, one with a snake's head terminal the other of thick twisted gold wire that holds a deep octagonal gold disk with a semiprecious stone setting. The snake bracelet is *circa* first century BC/AD, the other *circa* second/third century AD. Private collections.

Below left: Pair of openwork gold bracelets holding a central medallion with a facing bust of Sarapis in relief. Alexandrian work, *circa* first century BC/AD. Private collection.

Above: Pair of second-century gold earrings. Found at Granada, Spain. British Museum, London.

Below left: Fourth-century silvergilt fibula with a schematic horse's head and a Christogram picked out in dots on the circular plate. From Sussex. British Museum, London.

Below: Gold crossbow brooch found at the Moray Firth, Scotland, in 1847. British Museum, London.

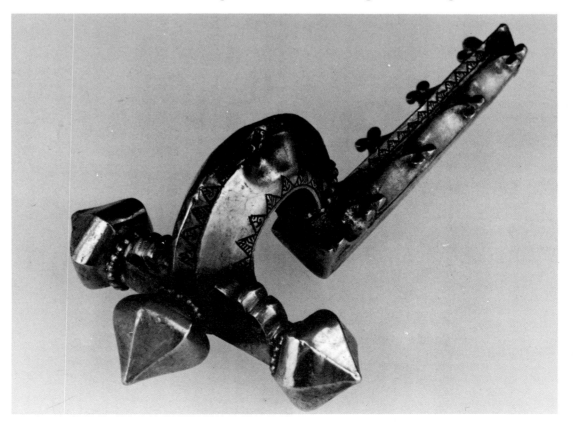

they were dealing, since they also wore rings. Pliny suggests that whoever it was who introduced the wearing of rings did so with some hesitation since 'he placed this ornament on the left hand, the hand which is generally concealed.' It transferred to the right hand when it was found to be an inconvenience while handling a shield with the left hand. Even senators only wore iron rings, not gold ones, for many years, some of the more old fashioned ones never adopted them. In the early days of the Empire rings were still a distinguishing factor among the different orders and classes of Roman society. How soon this changed we can see very easily from the mummy portraits of Roman Egypt. The wearing of several rings on an individual finger was not uncommon and they were not all worn pushed down over the second knuckle as nowadays. Roman ladies often wore small rings above the first knuckle, which were consequently quite easily lost. This is the explanation for the apparently high number of valuable rings found in small sizes which are invariably described as 'childrens' rings.' The number known is out of all proportion with the value of the ring which even doting parents would place on the hand of a small child. Some with atropaic symbols against the evil eye such as a phallus are indeed childrens' rings, but the majority set with intaglios and so on are from the hands of ladies of fashion.

In the late third and increasingly in the fourth and fifth centuries emphasis moved away from the gold setting of jewellery to an emphasis on the stones used themselves. Large heavy rings were set with carved intaglios and in many instances the gold ring was hollow over a core to give it strength. The art of the goldsmith goes into decline although a new form of goldwork became popular, *opus interrasile*, where the patterns were cut out of sheet goldwork with a chisel. This was a forerunner to its extensive use in the Late Antique period and Byzantium.

The largest hoard of associated late Roman gold rings, 22 in all, was only discovered in 1979 at Gallows Hill, Thetford, Norfolk (the silver spoons found with them have already been mentioned). They formed the stock-in-trade of a working jeweller rather than the contents of a wealthy woman's jewel box. As a group they bear out all the generalizations made about fourth century jewellery. Color is of importance in the settings so that even glass is used set in gold. Generally the goldsmith's work is not of a very high quality, it has a florid aspect suited to the period with its elaborate granulation and filigree. In pursuit of suitable stones for the settings it is interesting to note that all the engraved stones, the intaglios, are of an earlier period, and are being reused, even cut down as necessary. The art of the lapidary was in decline in the fourth century, not only could they not cut the stones so finely but they could not set them so well and often had to rely on an adhesive and backing material such as sulphur.

Generally speaking, Roman jewellery of the Repub-

Right : The 22 fourth-century gold rings found in the Thetford hoard, 1979. The goldwork is rather poor style and the intaglios set in several of the rings are of earlier date and reused. British Museum, London.

Above : Sardonyx cameo portrait of Augustus. The jewelled diadem is an addition made in the Middle Ages. British Museum, London.

lic and Empire is at a much lower level, both technically and in inspiration, than jewellery produced by other nations before them. There is occasional good work but it is rare. The jeweller-goldsmith only seems to come back into his own in techniques and inspiration with the later Byzantine styles.

One last aspect of Roman jewellery should be considered – cameo cutting. Small cameo heads on rings and the like are fairly common and range in date from examples found at Pompeii of first century BC/AD date down to a facing Medusa head in the Beaurains/Arras hoard of the late third century. It is in the large, pictorial representative cameos of the first century AD

that the Roman craftsman excelled. The technique used was one developed in the Hellenistic world. The essential ingredient is a stone such as sardonyx that has the property of layers of uniform but contrasting colors (or a piece of glass so layered could be used). High relief is a feature, leaving the darker color to act as a reflective background. Several portraits of Augustus and other members of the immediate Imperial family exist, and many of these pieces have been recognized as items of merit and have survived the centuries while being continuously known. A very fine sardonyx cameo of Augustus represents him in armor. Clever use of the darker background brownish stone brings out

the aegis of a facing head Medusa that he wears on his cuirass. Like so many of the fine early Roman cameos this one has been embellished in the Middle Ages by the addition of a jewelled diadem. Cameo busts of his wife, Livia, and his sister, Octavia, are known and are presumably both from the same school as the two ladies look remarkably alike.

Perhaps the greatest of the surviving cameos is the so-called 'Gemma Augustea' in Vienna. This piece is cut in onyx. The scene is in two registers and obviously refers to a great Imperial victory, although which one is not made quite clear. In the upper register Tiberius is seated on the right, the imperial eagle crouched

beneath his feet by a circular shield upon which he rests his feet. A wreath is held out above his head by a personification of the Mediterranean world. On a circular plaque before him is a capricorn. (This was Augustus' lucky sign, rather than his actual birth sign. He is said to have used this as his signet and it was a favorite reverse type on a number of his coins.) Seated at ease beside Tiberius is the goddess Roma, who turns toward him. To the left, an armored soldier stands beside a triumphal chariot that is proceeding out of the back of the picture leaving us to see the triumphator, crowned with a wreath and holding a long scepter, step down from the rear of the chariot. He is not in military dress but wearing a toga, although there is a helmet beneath the tailboard of the chariot (it probably belongs to the soldier). The features of the togate figure are not those of Tiberius so perhaps it may be Germanicus returned from the German wars. In the lower register the final gesture of victory, a trophy or panoply of arms is just being erected on a pole by struggling

soldiers. Barbarian prisoners, male and female, sit dejected beside the pole while to the right a barbarian chieftain wearing a torque around his neck (a mark of his rank) kneels in supplication and his sorrowing female companion is dragged forward by her hair. The male barbarians are certainly Celts, if not Germanic, and the episode must have been one of some consequence to merit so splendid a work of art. This piece was known and mentioned as early as AD 1246 in Toulouse and was kept there in Saint-Sermin until 1533.

The other great cameo, preserved in Paris, is the 'Cameo de France.' This is cut in sard and is the largest piece of this material known to have survived from antiquity. It was preserved from the Middle Ages until 1791 in the Sainte-Chapelle, Paris, since it was thought to have a Biblical significance, representing Joseph before Pharaoh. The proper interpretation of the scene is still open to question. It consists of three registers, the principal central band with Tiberius seated left greeting a standing armored figure who has been identified as one of several members of the Imperial family. Grouped about are probably other family members. In keeping with a triumphal return, the lower register shows a group of mixed barbarian prisoners. The upper scene is very enigmatic; it has been described as various divinities, but none appears to have any appropriate attributes by which to identify them. From the right a winged horse flies to the center, its rider going to greet figures flying from the left. One reclining figure holding a staff and wearing a draped radiate diadem may indicate that this is some kind of apotheosis scene, the translation of a member of the Imperial family to deification after their death. No doubt at the time this large piece was cut its symbolism and references were very obvious and well known. Lack of any definite pointers as to the subject, or possible literary references, leave us with room for speculation.

These large and specially commissioned cameos must have originated with the court but we have no idea as to their intended use or how they were presented. We can only admire them for themselves and leave them their mystery.

Left: The 'Gemma Augustea,' celebrates an imperial triumph but it is not a readily identifiable specific event. Cut in onyx. National Museum, Vienna.

Below: The 'Cameo de France' is the largest piece of sard that has survived from antiquity. Its principal figure is Tiberius, surrounded by various members of the Imperial family. Cabinet des Medailles, Bibliothèque Nationale, Paris.

Group of typical fine red ware
relief vases (and a head flask)
made in Roman North Africa.
The decoration consists of
appliqués made in gypsum
molds and attached to the vases
while in a leatherhard state
before firing. Private collection.

9. The Potter's Craft

Pottery is one of the commonest surviving manufactures of man after the so-called 'Neolithic Revolution' when he gave up his nomadic hunter-gatherer economy and became sedentary. He still had a long way to go to become civilized and a 'city dweller.' For the archaeologist, pottery is the great indicator of date, economic factors, trade and so on because, although pottery is easily broken, it is virtually indestructible. All civilized nations needed and used pottery. Rome was no exception although Roman pottery has always seemed to suffer from a bad press by being compared to the products of Greece and her colonies. The Greek pottery trade, first in Black Figure ware and then later in Red Figure dominated the Mediterranean. Greek colonists who sailed west to found the colonies of Magna Graecia (Greater Greece – South Italy and Sicily) naturally used pottery brought from Greece, but it was not long before very thriving industries began in southern Italy which used the techniques and followed the forms and decoration of the homeland. The indigenous pottery of Italy consisted of the rather heavy fabrics of the northern Villanovan cultures and the black glazed bucchero wares of Etruria. The Etruscans also copied the Greek forms and decoration but with their own style being readily apparent in their copies.

With such a plethora of types of pottery made locally, as well as the very fine imported Greek wares (and it should be remembered that almost all of the finest Greek vases in collections have come from South Italian sites), Rome did not have the necessary impetus to initiate a large pottery industry in Republican times. Coarse ware for everyday use was obviously needed and it does not stand out from the rest as being specifically 'Roman.'

Pottery is very much an individual product and each of the many nations that gradually became absorbed into the Roman Empire invariably had quite long traditions of potting, in its techniques, forms and decoration. As happened with religious spheres met by the spread of Rome, adaptations were made; each learned something from the other and no great startling changes were made overall. Hence it is not strictly possible to speak of 'Roman pottery' as such, rather of pottery of the Roman period from different areas. There are, in many instances, vast differences in basic popular forms, styles and techniques of decoration and finish between different parts of the empire, but there always was between some areas. As a case in point, typical Roman pottery from Britain bears no comparison with, say, the products of Roman North Africa, yet each is very much 'Roman' pottery and readily identifiable as such.

The epitome of Roman pottery for most people is the bright red, glossy 'Samian' ware. Red-gloss technique was brought to a high level by Roman potters in Italy

Left: A thick-sided pottery mold for a molded Arretine vase. The decoration consists of a series of 'kalathiskos' dancers and 'Pilemo,' the maker's mark can be seen (in retrograde to give a positive impression) in an oblong label by the bull's head. Metropolitan Museum of Art, New York.

Above: Footed Arretine bowl from the factory of Cn. Ateius featuring a procession of the Four Seasons; each is separated by a column surmounted by a satyr or Pan head, all elements of the design preserving a careful balance for the composition. British Museum, London.

(and later in Gaul) and it is necessary to examine the predecessors. The technique and manufacture of vessels from figured molds was in use in the eastern Mediterranean from at least the second century BC. Bowls, the commonest shape produced in this manner, were known as 'Megarian.' These were copied in Italy, often having the names of the potter concerned on them in Latin script. From these broad origins there arose a fine pottery industry based on Arretium (modern Arezzo) in northern Italy, which gave its name to Arretine ware. This was at first a black gloss ware which often had the names of Greek slaves working in the pottery impressed on it in Latin script. The implication is that the potters were from the east and brought their technical secrets with them. By the last quarter of the first century BC the potteries at Arretium had changed over to the preferred red-gloss technique and also introduced molded pottery. While with most pottery forms its ancestors can be identified as improvements which lead to better things, the molded Arretine ware almost bursts on the scene, already at a very high standard. The pottery is light, very well fired, figured, elegant in shape and crisp in decoration. The pottery factory of Marcus Perennius appears to have been among the first to produce this highly attractive, new-style pottery. A freedman of his who added his own name, Tigranus (redolent of eastern Armenian connections), to that of his benefactor may well have had a team of eastern-

trained potters under him. Among the signed molds from the factory is one by the workman Pilemo and his signature can be clearly read (retrograde in the mold, of course) amid the attractive decoration of 'kalathiskos' dancers and foliage. Such molds were produced by the use of stamps (*poinçons*) which themselves were of clay. They could be produced freehand by an artist or, more usually, were taken from a metal prototype. The stamps would be 'positives' in order to produce a negative impression in the mold and thereby a positive relief in the finished product. Quite attractive designs could be made up with the use of very few stamps. The areas in between might then be embellished with free-hand drawing using a metal stylus; this often produces recognizable 'signatures' of individual, yet unnamed, artists. When the final decoration of the mold was complete (which in many instances included working in the names of the artist-potter and the factory in small boxed areas) the whole was fired in a kiln. The product was a deep hemispherical bowl with rather thick walls. Once prepared the mold would be placed on a potter's wheel and very finely levigated (sifted and puddled) clay would be pressed into the intaglio impressions, keeping the inner skin smooth and relatively thin. If any kind of out-turned rim was required, it could be added and molded out over the top of the mold. The whole was then left to dry. In the drying process moisture leaving the clay would cause it to contract away from the mold side and so the 'inner' relief-molded bowl could then be lifted clear of its matrix, which was ready for reuse. Often such bowls then had a pedestal foot applied which much enhanced the shape of the vessel and the presentation of its relief decoration. The pedestal vase would now be ready to receive its distinctive red gloss. The red coloring is the product of iron oxides, hence only an iron-bearing clay would achieve the desired effect. The pot would be coated either by painting or by pouring the gloss all over it, or it would be dipped. Once the gloss was dry the pot was ready to be fired in a kiln, having been carefully stacked with its companions to ensure that the heat and air could properly circulate around the pieces. To achieve a good finish in terms of pottery quality, as well as the gloss coloring, a high temperature of between 1050–1200 degrees Centigrade was required. The resultant piece was a handsome object, as much prized in antiquity as they are now.

Decoration on these pedestal relief vases is always attractive and often incorporates figures such as the dancers mentioned or, as on a piece from the factory of Cn. Ateius, the Four Seasons. Such 'processing' subjects lent themselves to the shape and form of the pot without appearing to be repetitious. Mythological scenes are found from time to time, as are erotic scenes of pairs of lovers in various poses. The relief wares were the upper end of the market but there was also a very fine range of plain wares, of which the commonest is a shallow dish set on a low foot. They have remarkably clean lines, which makes them much appreciated today. Decoration at first was simple rouletting and subsequently molds were used to add a little tasteful decoration, sparingly used, around the outer wall, of S-curves or perhaps sporting dolphins. The maker's mark appeared impressed into the center in the form of a footprint (*in planta pedis*) with his abbreviated name within it. Many of the potters can be identified and Arretine ware, although it had a relatively short life (from early in the second half of the first century BC until the latter part of the first century AD) is quite closely dateable and a much appreciated chronological indicator for the archaeologist.

The Arretine ware factories began to decline in output during the second half of the first century AD and to give way to red gloss pottery produced in Gaul. The Gaulish potteries had begun their rise to ascendency earlier in the century, at first probably being staffed or at least directed by people from the Italian factories. The reasons for the Gaulish 'take over' were several: the product was actually of better quality than the Arretine, especially in terms of everyday use, it was of stronger fabric and better red gloss; and new or recently Romanized provinces needed 'Roman' pottery and the factories followed their best customers – the legions. So the Gaulish potters had every incentive, essentially commercial, and the first factories were set up in the area around Toulouse, especially at La Graufesenque and Banassac. The movement continued first to the northeast and then into central Gaul, where the great factory of Lezoux was located. All these factories were producing the red gloss pottery which is known generically (and incorrectly) as 'Samian' ware or *terra sigillata* (which is also incorrect to a degree because it is not always decorated). The name Samian arose because the pottery was once thought to have originated on the island of Samos in the Aegean Sea. Be that as it may, the names have become part of the archaeologists' and pottery students' vocabulary.

On the technical side, the color is obtained by the conditions in firing the kiln. Black samian ware is known (but is quite rare) and comes about by the pottery being fired in a reducing atmosphere. The more familiar glossy red ware is produced by being fired in an oxidizing atmosphere and the glossy finish or sheen is a product of illite, a mica, that is present in the clay. A good decorated Samian piece with a high gloss often looks as if it has been made from fresh red sealing wax. The presence of the illite in the local clays was therefore of major importance when setting up a factory.

Like the Arretine pottery, Samian ware often carried the potter's name (personal or factory) stamped into the center of the interior. From excavations on the sites of some of the major factories and also because study of the decoration indicates their origin in many instances, it has been possible to build up long lists of known potters and where they worked. The molds were produced in the same way as Arretine and the decorated

Above: Low-walled Samian ware bowl (form D.29) stamped by the manufacturer LICINVS. South Gaulish, *c* AD 35–60. British Museum, London.

Top: Deep globular Samian ware pot (form Dechelette 72) with decoration consisting of a combination of relief and *en barbotine* techniques. Central Gaulish, late second century AD,

found at Felixstowe, Suffolk. British Museum, London.

Top right: Deep Samian ware 'fruit' bowl (form D.37) stamped by CASVRIVS. Central Gaulish, AD 160–180. Found in London. British Museum, London.

Right: Fine red ware pottery flask from Tunisia with appliqué of a bestiarius attacked by a lioness. Private collection.

vessels made likewise. The difference between the north Italian and the Gaulish factories lay in the mass production required in Gaul. The potters needed vast numbers of molds since the waiting time before the pressed clay had dried out enough to shrink and clear the sides of its mold in a leather-hard state would seriously delay production if additional molds were not ready to hand for use. Not all decorated Samian ware had molded decoration. A rarer variant are the pots with incised decoration, usually a repeated floral motif, that was done directly onto the pot before firing. The idea was that it imitated cut glass and it is extremely effective; very rare examples of this type of decoration are also known in the rare black Samian ware. A list of the basic shapes and forms of Samian ware was drawn up originally by the German scholar Dragendorff (and later extended by other workers). References to shapes are usually by their 'D' number (Dragendorff), for example D37 is a well-known type of deep fruit bowl standing on a low foot with a band of relief molded decoration round the body and a plain band above it with a beaded lip above that. Fragments of Samian ware from excavations can usually be quite accurately identified as to their original shape by using such numbers. Around a hundred forms are identified by numbers but of those only about 10 of them are common decorated forms, the rest are a vast range of plain shapes, cups, plates, bowls and so on, and even mortaria and inkwells. Some of the plain forms actually have decoration on their rim which is not obtained by molding but by modelling. This is called *en barbotine* and involves a thick clay slip being squeezed onto the surface from a funnel, rather in the way that the decoration is made with icing on a cake. It generally takes the form of a running pattern of leaves and stalks.

Although Samian ware was a mass produced product it was the finer element of tableware and some remarkably fine pieces were produced. It was not cheap and the care taken of it is evidenced by the number of examples found that had been broken in antiquity and carefully repaired with rivets of bronze or lead.

In the same way that the factories at Arretium had declined, to be superceded by the Gaulish factories in the first century AD, history repeated itself in the second century with the decline of the Gaulish potteries and their place being taken by pottery factories in North Africa. Here, principally in the area of modern Tunisia, there must have been vast numbers of factories, judging by the quantities of pottery of distinctly North African fabric that survive. Like the earlier factories on the other side of the Mediterranean, they initially copied and imitated their predecessor's shapes and forms, then they broke away with their own products. Among the finer products of particular interest are the vases and flasks with relief decoration. The base fabric of the vessel is very fine and well levigated; the relief decoration is formed by clay being pressed into the appropriate small molds and then,

Above : North African red ware bowl with interior decoration of appliqués with a hunter and his hounds. Private collection.

Above right : Shallow red ware bowl with appliqué decoration, repeated twice, of the 'pastophorus' or Good Shepherd with a ram over his shoulders and a ram, each in a different stance, between the two figures. There is a clear Christian connotation in the subject. Private collection.

after slight drying, being peeled out and applied to the body when the pot is leather hard. It is then coated with its slip and ready for firing in the kiln. Quite amusing little scenes are often enacted on the applied relief vases, such as events in the circus, erotes rowing boats and rabbits leaping towards ferocious lions. Generally a vertically applied palm branch in relief separates the decoration into zones.

In later times, in early Christian North Africa, relief-decorated *lanxes* (large trays) became very popular. Their sources of inspiration lie in many instances in originals in silver and some parallels, like the Corbridge silver *lanx*, still exist. The symbolism and scenes on the trays and in relief bowls cover a wide spectrum of iconography. The life and deeds of Achilles are still a favorite motif, as has been seen on the great Kaiseraugst silver dish and in reliefs on sarcophagi. Pagan and Christian motifs often seem intermingled but it is the pagan element that has been adapted into the Christian scheme of things. Episodes from the Bible, both the Old and New Testaments, are very popular as relief decorations: Abraham and the sacrifice of Isaac; Jonah and the great fish; the children in the fiery furnace; the raising of Lazarus; and Christ as the good shepherd (*pastophorus*) carrying the lamb over his shoulders. The Christian community in Roman North Africa became very strong and produced, of course, such great theologians as St Augustine, Tertulian and others.

Among the very striking North African vessels are the orange ware head flasks, modelled in fine and often amusing detail. Some have faces that may still be seen in a Tunisian *souk* (market), others are idealized portraits of male or female. Most striking are the examples modelled as a satyr's head, complete with goatee beard and pointed ears. They are made in two-part molds and the handles added separately. Very individual in style, sometimes with an inscription in Greek or Latin incised into the funnel-like neck with a sharp instrument before they were fired, they are the Roman ancestors of the popular modern Doulton face jugs. Face jugs have always enjoyed a degree of popularity and while the Roman Tunisian pieces are perhaps at the top end of the scale, jugs and pots in the same idiom can be found far away on the northern frontiers in Britain. Pinched up clay faces occur on a number of pots from Colchester, Essex, made in the local kilns. They seem to have had some semi-religious function, one face has a pair of goat-horns indicative of the god Pan, and many were used subsequently as burial urns.

Left: Two very fine molded red ware head flasks of a young woman and a superb satyr, complete with pointed ears. Often such flasks have short inscriptions or names on the tall neck. Roman North Africa. Private collection.

Above: Head-pot found at York representing a lady with a hair-style well-known from the late second century as that favored by Julia Domna, wife of Septimius Severus. Yorkshire Museum, York.

A face-pot found in York shows a lady with centrally parted hair making her look rather like the Empress Julia Domna (wife of Septimius Severus). It was molded and then the features probably worked up with a spatula while it was leather hard.

In Gaul and Britain there was quite a tradition of pottery with relief molding. The Gaulish tends to be rather a heavier fabric and is often embellished with erotic scenes. The British is a finer fabric and comes mainly from the area of the Nene Valley, near Peterborough. It is called Castor Ware, after a small village on the north bank of the river Nene where, from the nineteenth century onward, quantities of this fine pottery decorated in the *en barbotine* style, have come to light. The kilns that produced it have been found all over the area. Strictly classed as 'coarse' ware, Castor ware pottery is far above the products of the normal local kilns. The decoration was squeezed onto the pot's surface, touched up as necessary and then the whole coated or dipped with slip before being fired to produce a color-coated ware. Favorite motifs were scenes from the hunt, rabbits or hares pursued by dogs around the pot in an animated but never-ending chase. These 'hunt' pots enjoyed great popularity in Britain although their origins lay in Gaul – they appealed alike to the Celtic population, who enjoyed hunting, and to the military. Similar *en barbotine* relief decorated pots were produced from the kiln sites surrounding Colchester (*Camulodunum*). One especially famous example is known as the 'Colchester vase.' On the principal side are modelled two gladiators in combat; one is a very heavily armed Samnite with a large crested helmet, its visor down, arm-guards, a short sword, rectangular shield and greave on his advanced right leg. His opponent is a *retiarius* who wears an arm guard on his left arm only since his main protection and weapons were a net and a trident. He has lost the trident, it lies on the ground at the Samnite's feet and therefore the *retiarius* is holding his right hand forward, index finger extended, to show that he is beaten. Incised inscriptions beside their heads indicate that the Samnite has apparently won eight victories and that the *retiarius'* name is Valentinus. It is not uncommon to find the names of well-known gladiators in the arena appearing on pots and on lamps. The next scene on the 'Colchester vase' is a pair of *venatores* (arena hunters), one of whom is partly armed and who is rushing along brandishing a long whip above the head of a very angry bear which turns its snarling head back at him. There are many similar scenes known in relief on the plates from North Africa. Here the two men are identified as Secundus and Mario. The third portion of the pot, the back, has an animal hunt in the Castor ware tradition represented in two tiers.

Glazed ware pottery was highly regarded and appears to have originated in the eastern end of the empire, where there was a long tradition going back to the ancient civilizations of the area. The vessels produced remained fairly small because of the problems of applying the lead glaze. The initial shape was first fired to a 'biscuit' consistency and then the glaze would be added. To keep an even color and depth of glaze was extremely difficult. Often the pieces would be fired upside down with a drip tray beneath them to catch surplus glaze that ran. Because of the technical problems involved lead-glazed pottery never achieved the widespread and common popularity of the glossy redware. Like the redware there is a tendency to copy shapes well known in metal, particularly the small two-handled cups still called by their Greek name of skyphos. The designs were usually floral, although some figure work is known, and the colors were yellowish on the interior and varying shades of green and mustard to brown on the exterior. Very elegant shapes taken from their metallic prototypes were much enhanced by the bright, gleaming luster of the lead glaze.

Lead-glaze-pottery techniques spread from the eastern empire in the first century, and factories for it

Top: Castor ware (Nene Valley) beaker with hunting scenes in relief of hounds chasing stags. British Museum, London.

Above: Nene Valley globular black beaker with applied scroll decoration in white. Found at Duston, Northants. British Museum, London.

Right: Lead-glazed flagon with relief decoration, an unusual and early import from Central Gaul found at Colchester. British Museum, London.

Left: The 'Colchester vase,' a superb example of a color-coated pot decorated with *en barbotine* relief scenes of gladiators fighting and a hunting scene on the back. Colchester and Essex Museum, Colchester.

Above: Deep two-handled lead glazed cup of 'scyphos' form with floral decoration in relief. Private collection.

are known in Gaul in the first and second centuries. Their products were not of the same quality and a number of examples found in Britain may well have been made there rather than being imports from the Continental factories.

One aspect or form of Roman pottery that is often overlooked or disregarded is the humble clay lamp. Very early lamps in the Middle East were just a shallow saucer with a slight lip against which a floating wick could rest. Developments brought a pinching in of the sides that produced the so-called 'cocked hat' lamp. The oil storage area was subsequently covered to make the lamps safer in use since a knocked or spilled lamp of burning olive oil could have disastrous results. By the later Republic, manufacturers in Italy had copied and refined the Hellenistic molded lamps from the eastern empire and late in the first century BC and the first half of the first century AD they began large-scale manufacturing. The distinctive feature is the nozzle, which at first was a very angular double voluted type. This gradually became rounded, then turned into heart-shaped, and then became simply plain and rounded. The shapes of the nozzles of Roman lamps are always a useful dating criteria. A large surface covering the oil storage area was now available for decoration and the opportunity was not lost to produce very fine and decorative motifs here, which is known as the *discus*. Some of these mold-made lamps are almost miniature masterpieces, certainly a large amount of information can be gleaned from them about Roman life. The Italian factories literally flooded the market with their products, exporting to virtually every corner of the empire. It was not long, however, before provincial factories set up and either copied the Italian originals directly or began to make their own quite distinctive products. They confuse matters by taking an original

Italian product and molding it, even sometimes down to the original maker's name, which appears as an impressed stamp in the underneath of the base. There is always a certain loss of definition in the copies and they are also smaller by virtue of shrinkage in the copy molded from the original. Like the Samian ware potters' stamps, those of lamp makers can often be traced and associated with particular areas where the factories were obviously located.

The subjects represented on the lamps provide a vast repertoire. On the earlier and large examples great detail is often found. The circus arena and amphitheater are extremely popular motifs. One example shows a very ingenious bird's eye view of a chariot race taking place in the Circus Maximus in Rome. The oblong shape of the circus has been constricted into the circular area available of the discus to show the spectators in their seats on the left and the right side has the four archways with latticed doors where the chariots enter. In the center, galloping around the central oil hole, are four quadrigae (four-horse chariots), moving at great speed. Artistic license by the mold-maker has moved the *spina* (the long low wall that divided the course down the middle) to the lower part of the lamp by the nozzle. Even here there is still an accurate representation, because he has shown the obelisk that stood on the *spina* which Augustus brought from Egypt in 10 BC and which now stands in the center of the Piazza del Popolo in Rome. Other lamps figuratively continue the story in showing the victorious charioteer parading triumphantly, carrying his victor's palm and with his supporters.

Gladiatorial scenes illustrate the different types of participants in the combats that have been seen represented in other media. Occasionally the names of popular heroes of the gladiatorial displays appear on the lamps. Other aspects of entertainment are not quite so boisterous where we see an entertainer, perhaps a juggler to judge from the hoops above his shoulder, practicing or training his animals. His tame monkey taps him on the arm while on his other side a cat is climbing up a ladder.

Among interesting topographical views are some lamps that show a harbor scene. There is quite a lot of detail on some of them and arguments have been put forward to identify them as the harbors of Alexandria or Carthage (it is probably the latter as the lamps all appear to be of North African manufacture). Some buildings on lamps can be identified with reasonable accuracy; one shows a mule cart being driven over a bridge to what is probably a public baths and this could well be the great baths of Antoninus at Carthage because literary sources mention just such an access to them.

All aspects of daily life, mythology and religion can be found on the lamps, including subjects which may not find a ready exhibition in museum displays nowadays, such as those with erotic scenes. These vary tremendously from the mythological erotic, such as Leda and the Swan, through what must be public exhibitions (often, incidentally, incorrectly recorded as being for use in brothels to go with the explicit wall paintings there), to simple lovers.

The North African lamp industry expanded alongside the pottery industry that had taken over from Europe and it produced huge quantities of lamps of very varied quality and subject matter. Some of the makers were extremely prolific and their names and products are very well known. An interesting change in forms and representations took place in the area toward the end of the period under consideration. Christianity had secured a strong foothold and the lamps changed in the late fourth and early fifth century into large red ware pieces made in a two-part mold.

The upper mold is highly ornamented, the lower has just a simple low ring base. Christian symbolism becomes very important, principally the chi-rho monogram, or Christograms; the fish, lamb, and doves; episodic scenes like those on the *lanxes* from the Old Testament; Christ himself standing holding his staff or, extremely rare, the bust of Christ on the center of the discus surrounded by 12 heads or busts representing the Apostles. Most of the lamps with very explicit Christian symbolism were never used. They were made solely for burial in the tomb and never lit.

Once more, it can be seen with decorated pottery and lamps that many of the motifs employed are the same as those used in other media or directly copied from them, especially from metalwork prototypes. Roman pottery is often regarded as a mundane product of the Roman world and its civilization – it is not. Principally it is the strongest chronological indicator that the archaeologist can find on a site and there are certainly many masterpieces among the thousands of pots that survive. Clay, as much as stone or metal, can lend itself to a master craftsman's touch.

10. Glassware

Cups and shallow dishes in mosaic glass technique were made by fusing rods of different colored glass together and then slicing and grinding the block of glass to achieve the shape required and produce either a translucent or an opaque effect. The technique was especially popular in both Italy and the eastern Mediterranean in the first centuries BC/AD. Private collection.

The glass-making industry suddenly expanded beyond all recognition under the Roman empire with the invention of glass-blowing – it brought about a revolution in manufacturing techniques and therefore in availability of the product. Pliny says in his *Natural History* that glass making was discovered by accident in Syria at the mouth of the River Belus where it enters the Mediterranean not far from Ptolemais (Acre). The sand in the river mouth was particularly clean and the story went that some sailors moored there and began to prepare their meal on shore. Finding no stones upon which they could balance their cauldron over the fire they had lit, they took some blocks of nitre (saltpetre) from their cargo and used them as supports for the cauldron. Once the fire got going the heat combined with the nitre and the sand and they observed 'transparent streams flowing forth of a liquid hitherto unknown: this, it is said, was the origin of glass.' It is a story that has a certain amount of credibility as regards the ingredients if not in the action that brought the glass about.

There does not appear to be any glass known before about 1500 BC. The two earliest dateable objects available are a small Egyptian goblet and a jug, each bearing the prenomen of Men-kheper-ra (the pharaoh Tuthmosis III, 1504–1450 BC) in a cartouche fired on with other trailed decoration in yellow, white and dark blue on a light blue body (they are respectively in the Egyptian collections in Munich and the British Museum, London). Certainly the invention of glass and the rise of the industry was in the Middle East, with Egypt and Syria in the forefront – a position that they were to maintain for centuries. Early glass was built up on a core, the commonest shapes being small unguent cosmetic vessels (such as alabastra and aryballoi) with trailed decoration in blues, greens, reds and yellows. They were very popular, as well as costly, and were widely traded, reaching into South Russia and Gaul.

The Hellenistic age brought a new impetus to the industry with an emphasis on mold-made shapes such as pillar-molded bowls that were especially esteemed in the West and widely found on first century BC/AD sites. The Egyptian glass industry came back into the fray with a rush after the founding of Alexandria by Alexander the Great in 332 BC and took a foremost part in providing plain and ribbed bowls in green, blue, brown or colorless glass (the last was at first rather difficult to achieve). With Pompey the Great's eastern conquests, Rome, hitherto a big customer for the glass factories' output, became the owner (Octavian/Augustus took Alexandria on 1 August 30 BC). Bowls made of mosaic glass were also a notable product of the Alexandrian glass workers, either made up by sections of polychrome glass rods set in a mold or of varying sized pieces, plaques and strips, fused together and then cut and polished. These have occurred in Roman tombs in Italy from the third to the first centuries BC.

Above: Translucent green glass pillar-molded bowl of the first century AD. Private collection.

Below: The famous Portland Vase. British Museum, London.

When Rome became a major power in the eastern Mediterranean Republican Rome developed a taste for eastern luxury trade goods. Not only were items such as glass heavily imported into Italy, eastern workers began to make their way there to set up workshops in the last century BC. It is interesting to note that these migrant glass-workers changed their styles to more locally suited requirements but the underlying techniques and approaches to certain subjects still betray their origins in a number of pieces that can only have been produced in the northern empire, especially in the Rhineland. Epigraphic evidence (as against literary references) of the glass-workers' origins is very sparse but a Carthaginian citizen named Julius Alexander whose funerary inscription gives his trade as a glass-worker (*opifex artis vitriae*) was buried at Lyons in Gaul, a long way from his sunny home in North Africa.

The invention of glass-blowing in the first century BC was the most important event in the history of glass. It probably began in Syria, which takes us back to Pliny's statement about the general origin of glass there. The new technique opened up whole new vistas and markets in social classes that hitherto would have been unable to contemplate the purchase of glass. In a matter of about half a century the skill of glass-blowing had spread across the western Empire from its eastern parents. Blown glass was found at Pompeii and Herculaneum which therefore dates before AD 79 and quanti-

ties of fragments have been excavated from northern Gaulish (Germany) military sites of the mid-first century AD. An enormous repertoire of shapes was opened up. Many carry the names of their makers impressed into them, thus Frontinus is noted for barrel-jugs and Lucretius Festivus for unguent bottles, and the plotting of such finds on distribution maps gives a ready indication of the currency of such products and an indication as to the direction in which their factories lay.

The best-known example of Roman glass is undoubtedly the Portland Vase in the British Museum. As mentioned above, according to legend it was found in a sarcophagus just outside Rome. It is said to have been discovered in 1582 and has been recognized as a supreme example of the glass-worker's art ever since. It takes its name from the Duchess of Portland, who bought it from Sir William Hamilton in 1785. He had bought it from James Byres (a Scottish dealer living in Rome) about two years before for £1000 and sold it, together with four other antiquities, to the Duchess for £1890. In 1810 the fourth Duke of Portland lent the vase to the British Museum where, 35 years later, on 7 February 1845, a young madman smashed it into over 200 pieces. Restored by the end of the year it remained on loan until the Museum bought it in 1945. Over the years it has been much copied, principally by Josiah Wedgwood in his famous jasper ware, and the subject of a considerable literature as to the interpretation of the scenes on it.

Originally the Portland Vase was an amphora shape, it came down to a pointed, possibly button-ended base. At some time in its life the pointed base was cut off and a similar-style cameo roundel substituted as a base. This shows the head of a young man (? Paris) but comes from a different object. The body and handles of the vase are from a dark cobalt-blue, almost black, glass and the relief decoration is an opaque milky-white glass. The vase was blown to its original amphora shape and cased with the opaque white glass which was then cut, cameo-fashion, in relief. Both handles are attached to blue glass at the neck (with no apparent joint) and to white glass at the shoulder, where a goat-like mask of the god Pan hangs beneath each of them. A lot has been written regarding the identification of the scene depicted, divided as it is by the Pan masks into two, yet it all relates to a single subject – the encounter of a young man with his lady love. The problems arise when any attempt is made to identify the several participants. Of the theories put forward, that published by Denys Haynes seems generally accepted as fitting the sequence of figures and placing them in a compatible myth. It is the story of Peleus and Thetis. Briefly, the brother-gods Zeus and Poseidon both fell in love with the young sea-goddess Thetis. Their ardor and interest was, however, rapidly cooled when Themis, goddess of order, prophesied that any son of Thetis was destined to be greater than his father. It was therefore agreed that she should be married to Peleus, son of Aiakos, the best of mortals. The resulting son was indeed to prove to be greater than his father, he was Achilles, the Greek hero of the Trojan War. Thetis is represented reclining in the center on what might be a rocky shore or in her sanctuary on the coast of Thessaly. The torch that she has used to guide her through the darkness hangs down from her left hand. Peleus, however, has been waiting for her and sits at ease gazing upon her beauty. The semidraped female figure to the right, holding a tall scepter, is presumably invisible to them both. She is Aphrodite, queen of love, who is just watching to see that all goes well and she also seems to be gazing rather pointedly at the flying cupid in the second scene, beyond the seated Peleus. The other side represents Peleus approaching Thetis, a flying cupid leads him forward, and she reaches out to clasp his arm while she has a sea-dragon, emblem of her home environment, beside her. The encounter is watched by Poseidon (or he may be Oceanus, her father) who stands resting his right foot on a stone and his head on his hand, between two trees. He seems to be contemplating the outcome, no doubt weighing up the prophesy.

The subject matter was obviously deliberately chosen and the Portland Vase was probably commissioned as a rather special wedding present for a young couple. Its size and high value would not have made it a very utilitarian object; like a lot of the silver of the same period (late first century BC/early first century AD) it was intended only for display. The wedded bliss

Above right: Mold-blown cup from Colchester with three registers or zones of decoration, the upper with the charioteers' names, the center with the *spina* of the circus and the lower with the actual chariot race depicted. British Museum, London.

Right: An elegant handled flagon and pillar molded bowl from Radnage, Bucks. British Museum, London.

inherent in the scenes made it a most appropriate gift, and one to be treasured. It was probably made in Italy but by a craftsman who was either of Alexandrian origin or highly skilled in Alexandrian techniques.

The Syrians were very adept at producing mold-blown vessels with relief decoration and they seem to have moved in force into, first, northern Italy, and then up into the western provinces, like the potters in order to be near their main customers – the Roman army, followed by the wealthy citizen-merchants who 'followed the flag.' A particularly interesting mold-blown cup was found in a cremation burial at Colchester, Essex. Made of olive-green glass it has decoration in three horizontal zones. The first, the upper, carries an inscription: HIERAXVA OLYMPAEVA ANTILOCEVA CRESCESAV. In the second is shown the *spina* that ran down the center of the circus, the triple turning posts (*metae*), obelisks and so on, just as is found on a number of sarcophagi reliefs and on the discus of lamps. The lower band or frieze shows four quadrigae racing. Three of the charioteers' names given in the upper band are followed by VA, presumably *vale* (farewell), while that of Cresces is followed by AV, presumably *ave* (hail), for he is the victor over the other three. The piece could not have been made in Colchester since it dates from the mid-first century AD and glass-making at Colchester is not evidenced before the late second or early third century AD. The cup was probably made in the Rhineland and imported into Britain so the scene cannot be interpreted as one of a race at Colchester, although the names of the charioteers might well have been popular favorites and well known in Gaul.

Below: A beautiful example of the glass workers' art; a large patella cup, *circa* late 1st century BC. Private collection.

Above: A fine example of a mold-blown beaker in translucent bluish-green glass of the late first century AD from the Syrian area. The decoration consists of four standing figures representing Poseidon, Summer, Dionysus and Autumn. Private collection.

183

Very elegant and valuable pieces of glass made their way safely across hundreds of miles to outposts of the empire and then, despite their obviously high value, were consigned to the afterworld with a burial. The splendid deep-blue pillar-molded bowl with white marbling found with a cremation burial at Radnage, Buckinghamshire, is one of the finest of its kind. The final finish on the interior and exterior of its deep rim was achieved by grinding and polishing. Another extremely elegant piece from Roman Britain is the tall olive-green glass flagon found at Bayford, Kent. This has two handles on opposing sides of the elongated neck, one much higher than the second and each with a trailed, blobbed tail passing down the wall of the flagon. It dates from the early second century AD.

Blown glass, although it could obviously produce so many different shapes quite easily, was still often used in conjunction with molds to produce special effects or elaborate pieces. An effective combination of silver and glass was achieved by a glass-blower who skilfully blew a cobalt-blue beaker into a silver casing which had over 60 oval openings spaced around it in eight rows. They diminish in size from the shoulder to the base and out of each the glass makes a gentle bulge. It really is a *pièce de résistance* and must have been a special order. Here the constriction of the silver case acted as the molding agent. Another blown and molded *chef-d'oeuvre* is a small pale green head-flask of a Nubian, of which less than six examples are known. This was made in a tripartite mold. The detail is so clear that the piece was evidently one of the first to be made from this particular mold. It is a very human representation, well studied by the mold-maker to reproduce the slight frown, parted lips and intense gaze of the eyes. Such a piece could only have been made in an eastern Mediterranean workshop, probably sometime in the late first or early second century AD rather than later.

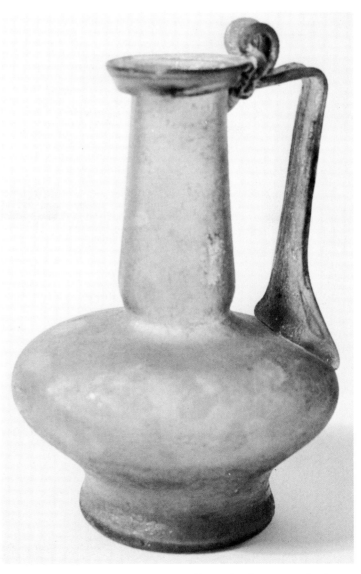

Above: An elegant small pale green glass handled flagon, probably made in Syria and found in Bath, Somerset. Private collection.

Far left: Into a silver beaker-shaped casing with over 60 oval openings a glass-blower skilfully blew a cobalt-blue beaker so that the glass gently protrudes through all the ovals. British Museum, London.

Left: Blue-green trefoil-lipped and handled glass jug from the eastern Mediterranean. Private collection.

Right: Heavy glass cinerary urn of a type popular for holding cremation burials in the second century. Private collection.

Opposite: Colorless glass 'snake-thread' flask, its ovoid body decorated with 'snake' trails and set on a low foot. Found at Aachenerstrasse, Cologne, and made in the area. Private collection.

Greens and greenish blue are the commonest colors found in most Roman glass from any area of the Empire because of the iron that is contained in the sand that forms its main ingredient. The clear colorless glass was difficult to achieve and tended to come from Alexandria. Plainer forms following the basic pottery shapes of useful dishes, plates, jugs and ewers, came within the reach of the middle and merchant classes. Glass could even be used for cremation burials. Many made use of the large four-sided and strap-handled jugs for this purpose, which has served to preserve a quantity of them for posterity. Globular, bulbous forms were made especially for use as cinerary urns, usually having a pair of heavy handles added and a flat lid with a knob (frequently the lid does not survive). This type of glass is generally thick and very heavy with a substantial rolled rope foot.

As mentioned previously, apparently Syrian glass-workers made their way into the northwestern provinces, northern Gaul and Germany especially, taking with them the techniques of their homeland. One of these was that of producing colorless 'snake-thread' trailed flasks from about the late second century AD. The ovoid bodies of the vessels have the corrugated trails winding round them, reaching up toward the tall neck where they usually stop at its base. Most examples are set on a low pad foot although occasionally they have a short stemmed base. Few survive intact because they are so fragile but a number have been found in the area of Cologne. Painted glass cups of the later fourth century, with their designs in enamel paint, were also a popular Rhineland product. They showed the wild beasts featured in the circus in lively movement racing round the cup. Curiously, all the best examples have been found beyond the frontiers of Rome, principally from graves in Denmark where they must have been especially appreciated.

Perhaps the greatest triumph of the Cologne glass factories are the *diatreta* (cage-cups). Their elaborate design and fragile nature ensures that very few survive intact. Once again, their origin appears to lie in Alexandria but the German workshops developed the technique. They were produced by first casting a thick blank and then wheel-cutting and grinding away at the surface following a traced out pattern, undercutting it and leaving it as a raised openwork pattern merely supported by a few cross pieces to the main body. The body is normally colorless and the casing is colored, including red, green and yellow. An example in Cologne from a grave at Köln-Braunsfeld, dated early in the fourth century AD, has a Greek inscription in red glass in the casing around the neck. The final effect was that of an inner vessel sitting easily within a network of glass threads that stood proud of its surface. The failure rate must have been enormously high and the cost of such pieces meant that they were the prerogative of only the very richest.

Cage-cups fall into two groups, those as just described

Above: Glass tracery cup or *diatreta*, an extremely rare example of a piece that the Cologne glass factories excelled in producing. Römisch-Germanisches Museum, Cologne.

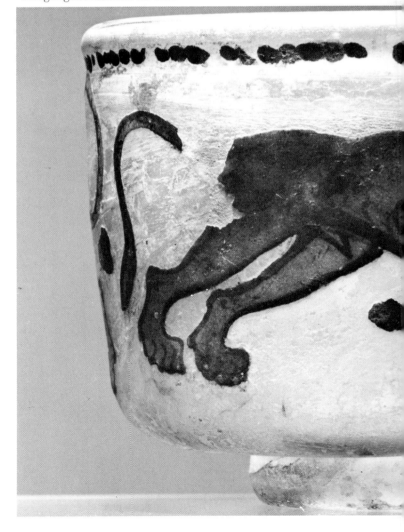

with network or pattern decoration and a second group with figured decoration. A fragment of the latter group is a cup that travelled very far from its place of manufacture, the famous piece found at Begram in Afghanistan which shows Neptune standing on top of what is suggested to be the famous lighthouse at Alexandria, one of the Seven Wonders of the Ancient World.

Undoubtedly the finest cage-cup of the figured type extant is the Lycurgus Cup in the British Museum. It is unique in combining elements from a myth with the *diatreta* technique, and also for its charismatic color properties. Like other cups of this type it is dated to the fourth century AD, although some would suggest a date early in the fifth century. As usual it was worked from a cast blank (which may have been mold blown) by wheel-cutting and grinding to produce the openwork. Its foot and part of the rim are missing (the metalwork on it being a later addition). The basic color of the glass is a cloudy pea-green, although a large part of Lycurgus' body and the legs of the maenad Ambrosia below his left hand, together with the adjacent vine tendrils, show as a yellower color. By transmitted light the vase changes color; the green turns to a wine color and the yellower areas to amethyst-purple. This unusual property in the glass is probably due to its containing a small percentage of manganese and colloidal gold.

The story unfurled around the cup is the death of King Lycurgus of Thrace. He persecuted the god Dionysus and his cult in his kingdom which was the area of the Edoni tribe in northern Thrace. Having chased the god into the sea with an axe, Lycurgus next turned on his attendant maenads. One, Ambrosia, stood against him and prayed for help from Mother Earth, who changed her into a vine which began to entangle the king in its branches. As he began to choke he still shouted defiance at Dionysus, who now appeared carrying his thyrsus and accompanied by his panther; a satyr who is about to retaliate and hurl a stone at Lycurgus, and a goat-legged Pan figure are all depicted around the cup. The whole scene is one of violent movement with three episodes of the legend shown in swift succession. What brought about such a commission we shall never know, or the master who created it. Together, and some 300 years apart, the Lycurgus Cup and the Portland Vase are examples of the finest glassware, in both technical and creative terms, that the Roman world produced. The eastern Empire continued its long tradition of manufacturing and innovation, new forms and decorations became current that took notice of the requirements of the new religion, Christianity. Gilded glass, which had been used only infrequently under Rome, notably in the fourth century, and later by sandwiching gold between two sheets of glass, was to find greater acceptance in the Byzantine world and reach great heights later under Islam as gold enamelling on glass.

Below: Cylindrical glass cup of 'Nordrup-Jesendorf' type found at Himlingoje, Denmark, and made in the Rhineland. The animal decoration is painted. Danish National Museum, Copenhagen.

Above: The finest extant example of a figured cage-cup is the Lycurgus Cup that tells the story of the death of King Lycurgus, struggling in the grip of a vine. British Museum, London.

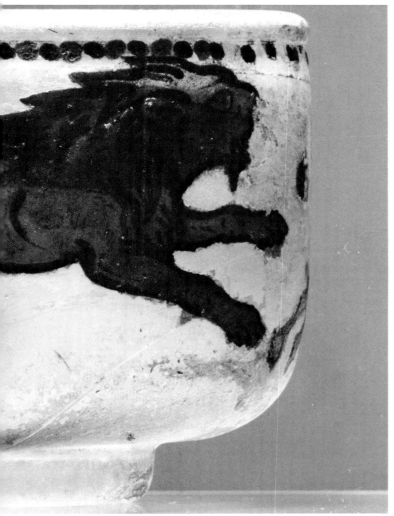

Index

CREDITS

The publisher would like to thank the following people who have helped in the preparation of this book: Adrian Hodgkins, the designer; Jane Laslett, the editor; Wendy Sacks, who did the picture research; and Penny Murphy, who prepared the index.

Anderson-Giraudon: pages 79, 116–17, 186.
Antiken Museum: pages 72, 130 (top).
Archivi Alinari: pages 13, 28 (below), 70, 83, 94 (top), 141 (bottom), 164.
Biblioteca Apostolica Vaticana: pages 12 (below), 119 (top right).
Bibliothèque Nationale, Paris: page 165.
British Museum: pages 121 (top right), 130 (bottom), 132 (center right), 133 (all three), 134 (bottom left), 135 (bottom), 136 (top left, center and bottom), 137, 141 (top), 145 (right), 149, 161 (top, and bottom right), 162, 163, 169, 176, 177 (top, both), 180 (bottom), 182 (both), 184, 189 (top).
Christie's: pages 15, 166–7, 172–3.
Christie's Colour Library: pages 147, 178–9, 183 (both), 187.
Peter Clayton: pages 18–19, 50–1, 12 (top), 15 (all four), 16 (both), 17, 20 (below), 21 (both), 22, 28 (top), 29, 30–1 (all three), 38 (top), 39 (both), 40 (top), 42–3 (all three), 45 (both), 46 (both), 47 (both), 49 (both), 54 (both), 55 (both), 60 (both), 63 (bottom), 64 (left), 68 (below, both), 69, 76 (left), 82, 86 (top), 87, 95 (left), 102, 121 (top left, center left, bottom both), 128 (top left), 131 (top), 134 (bottom right), 143 (top center, and bottom), 140 (top left), 150 (right, top two), 151 (top), 161 (bottom left), 170 (both), 171 (both), 172 (top two), 174 (both), 175 (top right, bottom), 177 (bottom three), 180 (top), 185 (both).
Danish National Museum: pages 8 (both), 9, 128 (center and bottom), 189 (bottom).
Deutsches Archäologisches Institut, Rom: pages 24, 25 (both), 27, 92 (left), 93 (bottom), 98, 104 (top), 109 (top right).
Hirmer Fotoarchiv: pages 120, 150 (right, bottom two), 151 (bottom four).
Institute of Archaeology, London: page 32 (top).
Istanbul Arkeoloji Müzelerini: page 148 (top left).
Kunsthistorisches Museum, Vienna: page 156.

Louvre, Paris: pages 64 (right), 74 (left), 94 (bottom), 112 (bottom), 113, 114, 115, 127 (bottom), 140 (right), 144 (left), 150 (top left), 159 (top, photo M Chuzeville), 159 (bottom).
H. Mahboubian Collection of Ancient Art: page 96.
Mansell Collection: pages 1, 14, 23 (both), 48 (both), 53, 56 (top), 57 (both), 58–9 (all five), 61 (bottom), 62, 75 (both), 78, 79, 86 (bottom), 91, 95 (right), 97 (both), 99 (top both), 100, 101 (both), 103 (bottom), 104 (below), 106 (top and bottom right), 107 (left), 108 (both), 109 (top left and bottom), 112 (top), 116–17, 118, 119 (bottom), 122–3, 125, 126 (both), 127 (top), 128 (top right).
Metropolitan Museum of Art: pages 77 (Rogers Fund, 1903), 136 (top right, Cloisters Collection, 1950), 143 (top right, Purchase, 1966, funds from various donors), 158 (Gift of Edward S. Harkness, 1936), 168 (Rogers Fund, 1919).
Moroccan National Tourist Office, London: page 41.
Photoresources: pages 2–3, 7, 10–11, 88–9, 152–3, 35, 36 (both), 56 (below), 61 (top), 63 (top), 71, 80 (both), 81, 84 (both), 85, 92 (right), 93 (top), 99 (below), 103 (top), 106 (bottom left), 107 (right), 131 (bottom), 134 (center), 135 (top), 138 (right), 139, 148 (right), 149, 155 (left), 157.
Susan Raven: page 40 (below).
Rheinisches Landesmuseum, Bonn: page 148 (bottom left).
Rheinisches Landesmuseum, Trier: pages 38 (below), 65.
Roemermuseum Augst: page 132 (top and center left).
Römisch-Germanisches Museum: page 188 (top).
Royal Commission on Historical Monuments (England): page 68 (top).
Scala/Firenze: pages 20 (top), 111.
Sotheby's: pages 110, 140 (bottom left), 142, 144 (right), 146, 160 (both).
Sotheby's/C I Skipper: page 145 (left).
Henri Stierlin, Genève: page 138 (left).
Susan Walker: page 34.
Warburg Institute: pages 66 (bottom), 67 (both), 105 (both), 134 (top), 173 (right), 175 (top left).
Jason Wood: page 32 (below).